I0082785

Learning How To Be Gay

(Also Available in Hardcover)

Learning How To Be Gay

LESLIE F. CHIFFON

Quadrakoff Publications Group, LLC
Wilmington, Delaware
USA

ISBN: 978-1-948219-67-9

Printed in the United States of America.

The rainbow banner on the cover art, is meant to be emblematic of the pure white light of God, manifesting in a myriad of prismatic and diverse creation.

Contents

The Genesis of the Work —————————— xiii

Chapter 1
The New Gay —————————————— 1

Chapter 2
The Biblical New Gay ——————————— 9

Chapter 3
The True Gay ——————————————— 59

Chapter 4
The Purpose of Man ——————————— 85

Chapter 5
The Source of the Problem ——————— 103

Chapter 6
Unholy Assistance ——————————— 129

Chapter 7
The Means to the End ————————— 159

Chapter 8
The Out Crowd —————————————— 181

Chapter 9
The Gay Circuit ——————————————201

Glossary —————————————— 215

Bibliography —————————————— 233

The Genesis of the Work

And so it was a quarter to five, and here I was finding myself in a rather jubilant mood. Humming the melody of "Yankee Doodle Dandy," I was pondering the "wisdom" of those who insisted that George M. Cohan was actually born on July 4th because: "He ought to know, he was there—you weren't."

Seems I would actually be leaving on time. First dinner; and then Bridge for the entire rest of the evening. My own wife felt the need to actually make a date with me two weeks ago, so I simply could not be late.

Suddenly there was a knock on the door.

"Come in."

"Oh Hi Leslie, how are you?"

"Did I get you at a bad time?" Leslie asked.

"No; of course not. Please sit down. How can I help you?"

"Well, I wanted to discuss something with you."

"Shoot."

"I would like to make a wager with you." (*Right away this was a problem, as Leslie was known to never gamble on anything, unless it was a sure thing.*)

"What kind of wager?" I asked.

"Well, since you are never wrong..."

"It's not that I am never wrong. I just do not speak unless I believe that I can improve upon the silence. And by the way, I know all about that stuffed toy raccoon with 'Rebecca' embroidered on its chest."

"Oh— Well I have an idea. You see I wrote this book, but I don't know if it fits our company's standards, and so..."

"What kind of book?" I asked.

"Well that's just it. Before I tell you, I want to make a wager with you. If I can prove you wrong in *anything*, then you promise to take a good look at my book. If I cannot prove you wrong; then I will agree to donate my MS63 Fugio cent, to a charity for dotards, dimwits; or any other category of your choosing that begins with the letter 'd'."

"That serious huh?" (*At this point my curiosity was getting the better of me. But I saw no actual downside. And the proceeds from that Fugio could help... No, if that were an actual possibility, Leslie wouldn't even be here.*)

"Well—are we on?" Leslie asked.

“So if you can prove me wrong on something, then I will see to it that your work gets a good look at, with no promises beyond that. But if you fail, then you will donate your Fugio cent to charity. Is this the wager?” I asked.

“Precisely.”

“Okay Leslie, you are on.” (*Somehow, I felt certain that I was being conned here, but...*)

“Well, just for fun, I watched the entire 1955 season of the television show “*What's My Line*;” and...”

“And what?” I asked?”

“Well, I just could not believe how *gay* they all were. It was so obvious. I simply could not help myself; so I wrote an entire book about learning how to be gay.”

“WHAT? Have you lost your mind? Firstly, that was 1955; so there is no way that they would have had openly gay people on that show. That just wasn't done back then. Many a movie star's career was ruined, simply because of that allegation. And secondly, we are Bible based publishers and do not delve into those social areas—especially that one. And furthermore...”

“GOTCHYA!”

“What do you mean ‘GOTCHYA’?”

“I mean you lose.”

“Why do you say I lose?” I asked.

“Because you don't actually know, what *gay* actually means.”

“Of course I do, why it means...”

"No, that is *not* what it actually means. That is simply what many want you to *believe* it means, just because they say so. Here take a look."

Leslie then handed me a book.

After a while I looked up at Leslie and said: "I see."

1

The New Gay

In today's world, one would be afraid to even ask the question: "Why would I want to learn how to be *gay*?" But this is a question that needs to be asked, because everyone by design *should* be gay; and be gay at all times. Specifically; it is God's will that all of His children be gay. How is this known? Because He told us so, of course.

The idea of "gay" in any way relating to any type of sexual proclivities, is a relatively new one. As is the public declaration of one's sexual preferences, proffered as some type of a "badge of hono(u)r;" as though the same would be of any interest to any reasonable person; or even be considered anyone else's business.

But these are just words—right. It doesn't matter what you call a thing, as long as everyone knows what you mean—right. And they *are* just words—aren't they?

Words are *symbols* for *actualities*, or *quasi-actualities*; that are designed to produce a *reality* that is consistent with the actuality.

What does any of this mean?

> "*Actuality* can be defined as what exists, and thus is completely *objective*—'The thing is what it is; and *aint* what it *aint*.'
>
> "*Reality* is what we *believe* exists, or normally represents what is merely *subjective* or *perceived* actuality."
>
> "*Reality* is what is *perceived* or *believed* to be so. This is in contradistinction to *actuality*, which is what, (actually), *is* so. That which is a mirage, but is not known to be a mirage; represents a *reality* of water, with an *actuality* of "not water;" e.g.; sand. This *reality* of water will be acted upon by traveling a great distance, only to then ultimately find that the previous *reality* and the *actuality* are quite different; producing a new *reality* for this very same actuality.
>
> "The seemingly disproportional response by the "petty" person; is considered as such, because of the

> *different* realities produced by the *same* stimulus, (an *actuality*)."
>
> "One cannot "actually" ever "come back to reality," simply because for any conscious mind, one's reality is impossible to ever leave. This is irrespective of any similarities or differences between any given *actuality*, (that which exists); and one's *reality*, (perception), of this same actuality.
>
> "The correct but rarely used phrase would be to "come back to *actuality*;" but then of course the question arises as to come back to actuality from *where*? From one's *reality* would be the only reasonable response, here indicating that said reality is believed to be inconsistent with the actuality involved."[1.1]

Thus "words" are *symbols* for *actualities*, or *quasi-actualities*. Here *quasi-actualities* represent actualities in a sense, in that all know that these are not "actual actualities" but *fictional*. It is true and thus an *actuality*; that there are film recordings of a man wearing a cape who can fly in the air with no known means of propulsion. But all know that what this man is "capable of doing" is *not* an *actuality*.

The *purpose* of *words*, or perhaps better phrased *terminology*; is to describe an *actuality*, so that the recipient can obtain a *reality* consistent with this *actuality*. Since all act from *reality*, to the same extent that one's *reality* is *consistent* with a given *actuality*; it is possible to act in a manner *consistent* with one's will. And to the extent that that one's reality is *inconsistent* with a given actuality, it is likewise *not* possible to act in a manner *consistent* with one's will.

Most *lexicographers* are quite busy. In the "information age" in which we all live, new words, (including acronyms), are being born—it seems constantly. In fact, there is even much confusion with regard to acronyms; as many that have different "meanings," nevertheless utilize the very same letters.

Thus keeping up with this, is an immense task for lexicographers. But the one thing most *actual*, (non-politically correct), lexicographers will not ever do; is to *remove* a word from "circulation." Many politicians will often attempt this for "political correctness;" but these are merely self-appointed, and not actual lexicographers.

It seems that rarely, if ever; does any language contain a word with "100% synonymity" to another word in that very same language. Thus if and when any word should disappear; then the precise *reality* of that *actuality* which this word symbolized, is lost—and true lexicographers are fully aware of this.

The very same can happen, if and when the *universal understanding* of the meaning of an existing word dramatically changes.

This is more than the common usage of: "'*touched*' in the head;" as opposed to the correct:

"'*tetched*' in the head; or: "'*shimmied*' up the tree," (see Bea Palmer); as opposed to the correct: "'*shinnied*' up the tree." Here although the incorrect words are commonly utilized, the understanding of the actuality remains—at least among those who utilize these words incorrectly.

But if and when a word is *removed* from the lexicon, irrespective of the method of removal; then whatever *reality*; i.e.; understanding of an *actuality*; that particular word "used to" facilitate, is likewise removed. It is true that there are substitutes, but generally without exception, none is as precise as was the original word. Lose any word, for any reason; and lose the *precise* reality of that actuality which that particular word symbolized.

This "removal process" forms the basis for George Orwell's "Newspeak."

Once this happens; in order to restore the precise reality of that particular actuality; one must either: somehow *restore* the word to the lexicon, (if "officially" removed); *invent* an entirely new word; or *reclaim* the original meaning of the word.

It is unclear as to precisely *when* the word "gay" began to have any relationship to sexual matters, in the general sense; or in today's more specific usage. Many try to trace this much farther back that seems reasonable. This effort seems more like an exercise in "verbal pareidolia," rather than any serious etymological effort. [*Pareidolia* is the term to describe the process by which one "visually" sees the face of Jesus in a pancake.]

Gertrude Stein, purported author and poet, and an open homosexual; published a work circa 1922 titled: "*Miss Furr and Miss Skeene.*"

Following is a short excerpt of: "*Miss Furr and Miss Skeene:*"

> "To be regularly gay was to do every day the gay thing that they did every day. To be regularly gay was to end every day at the same time after they had been regularly gay. They were regularly gay. They were gay every day. They ended every day in the same way, at the same time, and they had been every day regularly gay."[1.2]

The full work of Stein is much longer, but *in-toto* simply represents more of the same. Thus Ms. Stein is believed by many to be the actual source of redefining "gay" as "homosexual."

However it must be noted that the title refers to two *women*. So assuming 1922 is an accurate date of the publication, in 1922 Ms. Stein decided that the word "gay" was to take on a new meaning; and it seems that that meaning was not gender specific at that time. [It should not be overlooked that Ms. Stein may not have actually "repurposed" the word herself, as history is not clear in this. But clearly her efforts in the *distribution* of this "new meaning," had tremendous success.]

And although today, this "new definition" of "gay" is becoming largely gender specific with regard to *males*, it can still refer to *females*;

although this usage is considered as *passé* by many, and thus tacitly discouraged today.

Perhaps this is because there is or was a paucity of non-derogatory words to describe this particular *male* actuality. After all; for women there some socially acceptable terms such as: *Lesbian*, *Tribade*, *Sapphist*; as well as an assortment of others. But for men, *homosexual* is not gender specific; and most if not all other terms tend to have negative connotations—at least to some degree or another.

It is also unclear *at this juncture*, (but not for long); as to precisely *why* this was done. Here the "this," refers to choosing "gay" as the "new word" to symbolize this actuality; rather than choosing some other word, or simply inventing a new one. Before this can be addressed however, that which may seem irrelevant at this time should, in the interest of intellectual honesty, nevertheless be addressed.

2

The Biblical New Gay

There are many opinions as to precisely how many times there are references to *homosexuality* in the Bible. Here again there is often the aforementioned "verbal pareidolia," by those who wish to *increase* this number of references as much as possible, in order to try and show: "How bad God thinks homosexuality is." But even with this extreme "verbal pareidolia" utilized, the fact is that none can even get close to the number of times the word "sin" appears in Bible translations—which is believed by many to be at least *four hundred* times.

Most reasonable people believe that there are actually only *seven* verses referring to homosexuality in the entire Bible. But the various *translations* in the various versions, are each a bit "different" in their representations of these seven verses. It must be noted that according to Strong; neither the word "homosexual," nor the word "homosexuality," appears anywhere in the entire King James version of the Bible.[2.1]

The first "reference," in order of Biblical occurrence, is in Genesis 19:1-5 (KJV):

"And there came two angels
to Sodom at even;
and Lot sat in the gate of Sodom:
and Lot seeing them rose up to meet
them; and he bowed himself with
his face toward the ground;

And he said, Behold now, my lords,
turn in,I pray you, into your servant's
house,and tarry all night,
and wash your feet,
and ye shall rise up early,
and go on your ways.
And they said, Nay;
but we will abide in the street all night.

And he pressed upon them greatly;
and they turned in unto him,
and entered into his house;
and he made them a feast,
and did bake unleavened bread,
and they did eat.

But before they lay down,

the men of the city,
even the men of Sodom,
compassed the house round,
both old and young,
all the people from every quarter:

And they called unto Lot,
and said unto him,
Where are the men which
came in to thee this night?
bring them out unto us,
that we may know them."[2.2]

Since this event takes place in Sodom, a presumption of something relating to homosexuality is simply *assumed* by many. After all, the English word *sodomy*, is derived from the name of this very area. Thus these passages represent the *lynchpin* of the often seen "religious views" of homosexuality.

And given the common understanding of the events that ultimately took place in Sodom, homosexuality must then be some type of "super sin" to God.

And of course in particular it is verse 5: "*And they called unto Lot, and said unto him, Where are the men which came in to thee this night? bring them out unto us, that we may know them*;" which "clearly proves" this to many.

Some other Bible "versions," take this theory a bit farther.

Following is Genesis 19:5, but from "*The Amplified Bible*:"

> "*and they called out to Lot*
> *and said to him,*
> *"Where are the men who*
> *came to you tonight?*
> *Bring them out to us so that we*
> *may know them [intimately].*""[2.3]

Note the inclusion of the word "intimately" in brackets. This word in brackets of course does not appear in the original text, and was added by the translators.

And here is the same Genesis 19:5, but here from the "*New International Version*:"

> "*They called to Lot,*
> *"Where are the men who*
> *came to you tonight?*
> *Bring them out to us so that*
> *we can have sex with them.*""[2.4]

The word translated as "Sodom" back in verse 1 is actually:

> "5467 Ç^{e}dôm; from an unused root mean. to *scorch*; *burnt* (i.e. *volcanic* or

> *bituminous*) district; *Sedom*, a place near the Dead Sea: - Sodom."[2.5]

Here it can be seen that the *literal* definition of *Sodom* or *Çᵉdôm*, has nothing whatsoever do with sexuality of any sort. Certainly many would attempt to raise the "fires of hell" as some type of allegorical meaning for *Çᵉdôm*. But as can also be seen above, (the only word after the : -); the *only* English translation in the entire King James Bible for *Çᵉdôm*, is "*Sodom*."

In verse 5, this aforementioned question: "*Where are the men which came in to thee this night*?" might seem at first to make no degree of sense. According to verse 1, these "*men*" are or were not men at all, as we were told in verse 1: "*And there came two angels to Sodom at even*." Could it possibly be that their "wings" went "un-noticed?" And neither did they arrive "*this night*;" but rather "*at even*."

The original Hebrew word translated here as "angels" in verse 1 is:

> "4397 mal'âk; from an unused root mean. to *dispatch* as a deputy; a *messenger*; spec. of God, i.e. an *angel* (also a prophet, priest or teacher): - ambassador, angel, king, messenger"[2.6]

As can be seen, *mal'âk* relates to *function* and not *structure*. Thus their *structure* as "*men*" is possible; although their *function* here is as *mal'âk*.

These "men," acting as *mal'âk*; were the very same men who were present when God informed Sarah and Abraham, who were quite elderly; that they were nevertheless going to have a child.

This is known, because in the previous chapter, here Genesis 18:16 (KJV), we are told:

"And the men rose up from thence,
and looked toward Sodom:
and Abraham went with them
to bring them on the way."[2.7]

And shortly after, in Genesis 18:22 (KJV), we are told:

"And the men turned their faces from
thence, and went toward Sodom:
but Abraham stood yet before the Lord."[2.8]

What was it that was "going on" in Sodom, that prompted God to send these "*mal'âk* men?"

Genesis 18:20 tells us:

"And the Lord said,
Because the cry of Sodom
and Gomorrah is great, and
because their sin is very grievous;"[2.9]

Here God describes the behaviors in Sodom as "*sin*" and "*very grievous.*"

The original Hebrew word translated here as "sin" is:

> "2403 chaṭṭâ'âh; or chaṭṭâ'th; from 2398; and *offense* (sometimes habitual *sinfulness*), and its penalty, occasion, sacrifice, or expiation; also (concr.) an *offender*: - punishment (of sin), purifying (-fication for sin), sin (-ner, offering)."[2.10]

> "2398 châṭâ'; a prim. root; prop. to *miss*; hence (fig. and gen.) to *sin*; by infer. to *forfeit*, *lack*, *expiate*, *repent*, (causat.) *lead astray*, *condemn*..."[2.11]

The original Hebrew word translated here as "grievous" is:

> "3513 kâbad; or kâbêd; a prim. root; to *be heavy*, i.e. in a bad sense (*burdensome*, *severe*, *dull*) or in a good sense numerous, *rich*, *honorable*); causat. to *make weighty* (in the same two senses)..."[2.12]

The original Hebrew word translated here as "very" is:

> "3966 m^e 'ôd; from the same as 181; prop. *vehemence*, i.e. (with or without

> prep.) *vehemently*; by impl. *wholly*, *speedily*, etc. (often with other words as an intensive or superlative; espec. when repeated)..."[2.13]

So what God is saying here is that those in Sodom have an "offense and its penalty," *chaṭṭâ'âh*; that is "vehemently," (*m*^{e}*'ôd*); "heavy," (*kâbad*). But God provides no information to us, as to what the *nature* of this offense or sin is. So there is no specific information provided in these passages; as to precisely *what* it is or was, they were doing or had done that was: "vehemently heavy."

And it seems that the group making this request or demand to Lot; was a rather large group of people. In fact, it seems likely that there was not even one person in the area who was *not* in this group; as we are told this group was: "*the men of the city, even the men of Sodom, compassed the house round, both old and young, all the people from every quarter.*"

But it should be asked if there were any females contained in this group. The word "*men*" appears twice: "*the men of the city*" and: "*even the men of Sodom.*"

The original Hebrew word translated as "men" here in verse 4; and also the "men" in verse 5: "*men which came in to thee this night,*" is:

> "582 'ĕnôwsh; from 605; prop. a *mortal* (and thus differing from the more dignified 120); hence a *man* in gen. (singly or collect.)..."[2.14]

Here it seems that *'ĕnôwsh* is more concerned with *mortality* vs. *immortality*; rather than the *gender* of the mortal.

And we are also told "*all the people*" were in this group.

The original Hebrew word translated as "people" is:

> "5971 'am; from 6004 a *people* (as a congregated *unit*); spec. a *tribe* (as those of Israel); hence (collect.) *troops* or *attendants*; fig. a flock: - folk, men, nation, people"[2.15]

And the stated purpose for the request or demand that Lot: "*bring them out unto us,*" was: "*that we may know them.*"

The actual Hebrew word translated as "know" is:

> "3045 yâda'; a prim. root; to *know* (prop. to ascertain by *seeing*); used in a great variety of senses, fig. lit. euphem. and infer. (including *observation*, *care*, *recognition*; and causat. *instruction*, *designation*, *punishment*, etc.)..."[2.16]

This word *yâda'* meaning: "a prim. root; to *know* (prop. to ascertain by *seeing*);" generally means what the definition states. However, *yâda'* is in fact sometimes used as a *euphemism* for sexual relations, as will be seen shortly.

Genesis 19:6-8 (KJV) tells us what Lot then does:

"And Lot went out at the door unto them, and shut the door after him,

And said, I pray you, brethren, do not so wickedly.

Behold now, I have two daughters which have not known man; let me, I pray you, bring them out unto you, and do ye to them as is good in your eyes: only unto these men do nothing; for therefore came they under the shadow of my roof."[2.17]

So in response to the crowd's demand, Lot leaves the house; and shuts the door behind him; and then offers his two daughters who: "*have not known man.*"

The actual Hebrew word translated here as "known," is also the above 3045 *yâda'*;[2.18] but here "not known (*yâda'*) man;" is seemingly used as the aforementioned *euphemism* for *virginity*. Clearly these two daughters *literally* knew, or: "*yâdă*"; a prim. root; to *know* (prop. to ascertain by *seeing*;" their father Lot—who of course was a "*man*."

So it must be asked precisely what it was that Lot was thinking.

If these men's "sin" was *homosexuality*, why would Lot believe that they would be in any way interested in two virgin females? Or is the argument, that since there may also have been homosexual *women* in the group, these might have had some interest—thus it *still* relates to homosexuality? Or is it just that plain old normal, (heterosexual), sexual relations that Lot is offering the group? Or is it something else?

Lot had lived in this area after choosing the valley, while his Uncle Abraham had chosen the mountains, after their "spat;" so Lot likely knew of the "goings on" in the area.

And in those times, it was likely that whatever the makeup of this crowd, it was a male who was doing the speaking to Lot. So *if* the statement: "*that we may know them*" represents the *euphemistic*; and not the *literal* definition of *yâda'*—just as Lot had just done; then it would seem that it was *males* that these speakers would have wanted, and not *females*.

So again, what was Lot thinking? Did Lot actually believe that these men wanted men; but that somehow giving them two females would suffice? Likely not.

The issue here is not sexual *promiscuity*.

The issue here is supposed to be *homosexuality*.

The truth is that these people in the crowd were very bad people. They were so bad that God was about to destroy the entire area. But we are not in any way told in these passages, precisely what their actual specific behaviors were, that prompted this grave decision by God to destroy the area.

So the *translators* merely *assumed*, (not *presumed*), two things:

Firstly, they assumed that it is proffering the *euphemistic* definition of *yâda'* that is taking place here, and not the *literal* use of *yâda'*. And furthermore, that these wicked speakers were actually telling the truth about this *euphemistic* meaning; rather than meaning the *literal* definition of *yâda'*, but lying about it.

And *secondly*, that this assumed homosexuality was both rampant, and "evil enough;" for God to destroy the entire area.

Lot "knew" these people; and thus knew of their moral bankruptcy. When he told them: "*do ye to them as is good in your eyes*," this was not a statement of exclusivity with regard to women only, to *yâda'* his daughters in the *euphemistic* meaning. Rather, Lot was offering his consent to the members of this crowd to do anything that they wished to his own daughters.

Lot likely also knew what the function of these two "*mal'âk* men" was to be. It was the duty of these two, to actually destroy this area as per God's wishes. So it was *Lot's* duty to protect these two "*mal'âk* men" from the crowd; who although proffered the desire to *yâda'* them in the *literal* sense; were in fact lying, and were actually planning to kill these two men.

What was the crowd's response to Lot's "offering?"

Genesis 19:9-11 (KJV) tells us their response:

"And they said, Stand back.
And they said again,
This one fellow came in to sojourn,
and he will needs be a judge:

now will we deal worse with thee,
than with them.
And they pressed sore upon the man,
even Lot, and came near
to break the door.

But the men put forth their hand,
and pulled Lot into the house to them,
and shut to the door.

And they smote the men that
were at the door of the
house with blindness,
both small and great:
so that they wearied themselves
to find the door."[2.19]

The key phrase in the crowd's response is: "*now will we deal worse with thee, than with them.*"

In English there are three degrees of comparison: Positive, Comparative, and Superlative. The word "worse" is the *comparative* of the *positive* "bad." In order to be a *comparative*, unlike is the case of the *positive*; there must be another word with which to *compare* it. Ergo; if whatever the crowd was going to do to Lot, ("*deal*"); was to be "*worse*" than what the crowd was going to do to the two men, as stated in this KJV translation; it is therefore required that whatever they were going to do with the two men to be "bad."

Many *heterosexuals* may consider *homosexuality* as "bad." But it does not seem that consensual homosexual activities would be considered bad by the homosexuals involved—else why consent?

The "*Interlinear Bible*" translates this phrase as: "*Now we will do evil to you rather than to them.*"[2.20]

The actual original Hebrew translated as "evil" in the Interlinear Bible is:

> "7489 râ'a'; a prim. root; prop. to *spoil* (lit. by *breaking* to pieces); fig. to *make* (or be) *good for nothing*, i.e. *bad* (phys., soc. or mor.)..."[2.21]

It must be asked if the *euphemistic* meaning of *yâda'*, as seen in the cited Amplified Bible translation: "know them [intimately];" and the NIV Bible translation: "have sex with them;" in any way comports with what the crowd told Lot they were going to do to *him*, (râ'a'); rather than the two men, as defined: "to *spoil* (lit. by *breaking* to pieces); fig. to *make* (or be) *good for nothing*, i.e. *bad* (phys., soc. or mor.)"

The crowd then: "*pressed sore upon*" Lot, and tried to break down the door. And the two "*men*," then: "*pulled Lot into the house to them, and shut to the door.*" These two "*men*" then made the crowd blind, so that they then "*wearied themselves*" trying to find the door.

A fair read of the "goings on" recounted in this *story*, (not parable); is that this story had nothing to do with homosexuality, except perhaps tangentially. These were wicked people for certain. They were so wicked God had no choice but to destroy them all. In fact in the previous chapter, after Abraham "bargaining" with God; God had told Abraham that if ten "*righteous*" were "*found there*," He "*will not destroy it*."[2.22]

One might fairly ask why this bargaining by Abraham with God that began with fifty, and worked its way down to ten, but then stopped there. Meaning: Why did Abraham not then try five, or one? The answer is that at the time of the actual destruction, in the "righteous" department; there would be present at a minimum: Lot, Lot's wife, the two "men angels," and Lot's two daughters. That is six, and God is not a fool.

Like "bacon and eggs," Sodom is usually associated with another city: Gomorrah (Old Testament spelling)—particularly when homosexuality is under discussion. In fact: "Sodom and Gomorrah," could be reasonably considered as a "quasi-euphemism" for homosexuality.

"Gomorrah" appears 19 times in the Old Testament.[2.23] And "Gomorrha" appears 5 times in the New Testament.[2.24]

The Old Testament appearances as "Gomorrah," are in: Genesis 10:19, Genesis 13:10, Genesis 14:2, Genesis 14:8, Genesis 14:10, Genesis 14:11, Genesis 18:20, Genesis 19:24, Genesis 19:28, Deuteronomy 29:23, Deuteronomy 32:32, Isaiah 1:9, Isaiah 1:10, Isaiah 13:19, Jeremiah 23:14, Jeremiah 49:18, Jeremiah 50:40, Amos 4:11, and Zephaniah 2:9.[2.25]

The New Testament appearances as "Gomorrha," are in: Matthew 10:15, Mark 6:11, Romans 9:29, 2 Peter 2:6, and Jude 7.[2.26]

No reasonable references to homosexuality could be found in any of these "Gomorrah" or "Gomorrha" passages.

And it seems that Sodom and Gomorrah were not the only cities destroyed in this manner; and destroyed on that very same day.

Jeremiah 50:40 (KJV) tells us:

"As God overthrew Sodom and Gomorrah
and the neighbour cities thereof,
saith the Lord; so shall no man abide there,
neither shall any son of man dwell therein."[2.27]

Deuteronomy 29:23 (KJV) tells us:

"And that the whole land thereof
is brimstone, and salt, and burning,
that it is not sown, nor beareth,
nor any grass groweth therein,
like the overthrow of Sodom,
and Gomorrah, Admah, and Zeboim,
which the Lord overthrew in his anger,
and in his wrath:"[2.28]

Genesis 19:25 (KJV) tells us:

"And he overthrew those cities,
and all the plain,and all the inhabitants

of the cities, and that
which grew upon the ground."[2.29]

Here "*those cities*" refers to Sodom and Gomorrah; while and "*all the plain*" refers to the other cities referenced: Admah and Zeboim.

The problem; is the impression that was left with the public for *millennia*, about the uniquely extreme level of "sinfulness" of homosexuality; i.e.; that homosexuality was the "unforgivable sin." During the time that Jesus walked the earth, there is believed to have been an unforgivable sin; but it was not in any way related to homosexuality.

Thus for millennia the public's *reality* of these passages remained and remains far in excess of the actuality provided by an unbiased reasonable read of the same. This reality/actuality mismatch, and its significance; will be addressed in further detail later.

The next two purported Biblical "references" to homosexuality, appear chronologically in Leviticus 18:22 (KJV), and in Leviticus 20:13 (KJV).

Leviticus 18:22 (KJV) tells us:

"Thou shalt not lie with mankind,
as with womankind:
it is abomination."[2.30]

Leviticus 20:13 (KJV) tells us:

*"If a man also lie with mankind,
as he lieth with a woman, both of
them have committed an abomination:
they shall surely be put to death;
their blood shall be upon them."*[2.31]

The original Hebrew word translated as "abomination" in each of these verses is:

> "8441 tôwʻêbâh; or tôʻêbâh; fem. act. part. of 8581 prop. something *disgusting* (mor.), i.e. (as noun) an *abhorrence*; espec. *idolatry* or (concr.) an *idol*"[2.32]

The "revelation" contained in these two verses, is that the author(s) of the same, believe that homosexuality is "something disgusting."

This is important because *disgust* is a *subjective* "feeling;" and not in any way *objective* in nature. The root of *disgusting* is the Latin *gustare*; and this root is also seen in the English word gustatory, relating to taste or tasting. The same *subjectivity* can be said for *abhorrence.*

We are not told in these passages that homosexuality is *wicked* or *evil.* These would be *objective* characterizations based upon, say; what God told Moses. This is ironic because much of Leviticus is considered to be what God told Moses.

It is unclear who actually wrote Leviticus; as is how long it took to write. And Leviticus is much more concerned with man's *behaviors*, than belief in God. Likely it was written by "lawyers," and thus arguably belongs in the *Talmud*; and does not belong in the "Torah."

The next purported Biblical "reference" to homosexuality, appears chronologically in Mark 10:6-9 (KJV):

"But from the beginning of the creation
God made them male and female.
For this cause shall a man leave
his father and mother,
and cleave to his wife;
And they twain shall be one flesh:
so then they are no more twain,
but one flesh.

What therefore God hath joined together,
let not man put asunder."[2.33]

It remains unclear precisely what, if anything, these passages have to do with *homosexuality*. "But" since these verses begin with a "*but*," this clearly indicates some type of *exception* to that which appears in the verse(s) *before* these verses.

Mark 10:2-5 (KJV) tell us precisely what it is that the above Mark 10:6-9, is the exception, (the "*but*"), to:

"And the Pharisees came to him,

and asked him,
Is it lawful for a man to put away
his wife? tempting him.

And he answered and said unto them,
What did Moses command you?

And they said, Moses suffered to write a
bill of divorcement, and to put her away.

And Jesus answered and said
unto them, For the hardness of
your heart he wrote you this precept."[2.34]

Thus it seems that Mark 10:6-9 has nothing whatsoever to do with homosexuality; but rather *divorce*; which although being inconsistent with God's will, divorce is necessary because of: "*hardness of your heart.*"

The next purported Biblical "reference" to homosexuality, appears chronologically in Romans 1:26-28 (KJV):

"For this cause God gave them
up unto vile affections:
for even their women did change the natural
use into that which is against nature:

And likewise also the men,
leaving the natural use of the woman,

burned in their lust one toward another; men with men working that which is unseemly, and receiving in themselves that recompence of their error which was meet.

And even as they did not like to retain God in their knowledge, God gave them over to a reprobate mind, to do those things which are not convenient;"[2.35]

The key statements in these verses: "*their women did change the natural use into that which is against nature;*" and: "*men leaving the natural use of the woman, burned in their lust one toward another; men with men working that which is unseemly;*" seem to clearly refer to homosexuality. Here "*natural use*" seems to be a euphemism for "normal" sexual acts.

However there may be a bit more wisdom available, as these passages begin with: "*for this cause.*" Thus whatever follows this: "*for this cause,*" are then necessarily the *results* of some *cause* that is unspecified in these verses. There is a *cause-effect* relationship being stated here; with that which is contained in these Romans 1:26-28 passages describing only the *effects* or the *results*.

The *cause* for these *results* that are described in Romans 1:26-28, should be contained in the passages which directly *precede* Romans 1:26-28.

That which precedes Romans 1:26-28, here Romans, 1:21-25 (KJV) tells us:

"Because that, when they knew God,
they glorified him not as God,
neither were thankful;
but became vain in their imaginations,
and their foolish heart was darkened.

Professing themselves to be wise,
they became fools,

And changed the glory
of the uncorruptible God into
an image made like to corruptible man,
and to birds, and fourfooted beasts,
and creeping things.

Wherefore God also gave
them up to uncleanness
through the lusts of their own hearts,
to dishonour their own bodies
between themselves:

Who changed the truth of God into a lie,
and worshipped and served the
creature more than the Creator,
who is blessed for ever. Amen."[2.36]

There are a lot of "really bad" things happening in these Romans 1:21-25 passages; which are the *causes*, ("*for this cause*"); for the *effects* or *results* described in Romans 1:26-28.

However, the only part of these Romans 1:21-25 passages that could seem to in any reasonable way relate to sexual matters; follows the "*also gave them up to uncleanness,*" and is: "*the lusts of their own hearts, to dishonour their own bodies between themselves.*" Thus this "*also*" necessarily means in addition to that which appears before the "*also.*"

But there is no indication of *gender* at this, Romans, 1:21-25, juncture. Thus if these words do in fact relate to sexual matters, it would seem that at least here, this would likely be the *horse*, (heterosexuality); and not the zebra, (homosexuality). Thus any and all "unnatural" sexual acts could seem to be what is being addressed; as well as that which is considered "natural," but *promiscuous* acts—at least here in these Romans 1:21-25 verses.

And the "*God also gave them up to uncleanness,*" merits some analysis; as this relates to something else contained in the Romans 1:26-28 passages, which purportedly relates to homosexuality.

The actual Greek word translated as "gave them up" is:

"3860 paradidōmi; from *3844* and *1325*; to *surrender*, i.e. *yield up, intrust, transmit...*"[2.37]

The actual Greek word translated as "uncleanness" is:

> "167 akatharsia; from *169*; *impurity* (the quality), phys. or mor.: -uncleanness"[2.38]

It might seem that that which is the *reason* referenced in Romans 1:26-28, as per the "*for this cause;*" is contained in these Romans 1:21-25 passages. It is because God "*gave them up,*" (paradidōmi); to "*uncleanness,*" (akatharsia); *in-toto*. Meaning that this "giving up," was because of that which appears *before*, as well as that which appears *after* this "*also.*"

If the *cause*, ("*for this cause*"), stated in Romans 1:26-28; for the *results* of the purported homosexuality contained in these same Romans 1:26-28 verses, were to relate solely to homosexuality; and related to none of the statements *before* the "*also the men;*" and none of the other reasons *after* the "*also the men;*" then these other reasons given seem superfluous.

In fact it is a more reasonable position that this "*the lusts of their own hearts, to dishonour their own bodies between themselves*" statement is not in any way the *primary cause*, but instead a *secondary cause* of this, (homosexuality), *result* contained in Romans 1:26-28.

Meaning; that all of the "bad things" described in Romans 1:21-25 passages *except*: "*the lusts of their own hearts, to dishonour their own bodies between themselves,*" were the actual *primary* causes; with the *result* of: "*the lusts of their own hearts, to dishonour their own bodies between themselves.*"

And it was the *result* of these "*lusts,*" that then became the actual *cause*, ("for this cause"); for the behaviors described in Romans 1:26-28: "*their women did change the natural use into that which is against nature*" and: "*men leaving the natural use of the woman, burned in their lust one toward another; men with men working that which is unseemly.*

Meaning; it: "went something like this:"

First: "*Because that, when they knew God, they glorified him not as God, neither were thankful; but became vain in their imaginations, and their foolish heart was darkened. Professing themselves to be wise, they became fools, And changed the glory of the uncorruptible God into an image made like to corruptible man, and to birds, and fourfooted beasts, and creeping things. Who changed the truth of God into a lie, and worshipped and served the creature more than the Creator, who is blessed for ever. Amen.*"

Then, and because of *these* actions: "*Wherefore God also gave them up to uncleanness through the lusts of their own hearts, to dishonour their own bodies between themselves.*"

And then, and because of these "*lusts;*" then "*their women did change the natural use into that which is against nature*" and: "*men leaving the natural use of the woman, burned in their lust one toward another; men with men working that which is unseemly.*"

A fair conclusion is that these Romans 1:21-25 passages are primarily concerned with *idolatry*; with perhaps some type of sexual: "*dishonour their own bodies between themselves,*" first of an unspecified, (possibly heterosexual or homosexual), nature as a *result*.

Then there is the "final" *result* of: "*their women did change the natural use into that which is against nature*" and: "*men leaving the natural use of the woman, burned in their lust one toward another; men with men working that which is unseemly,"* which is contained in Romans 1:26-28.

First: "*their women did change the natural use into that which is against nature.*"

The original Greek word translated as "change" is:

> "3337 mĕtallassō; from *3326* and *236*; to *exchange*: - change."[2.39]

As can be seen, *mĕtallassō* means *exchange*; yet the translation is *change*. There are major differences.

When one *changes* something, generally one alters a "thing" to have characteristics different than the characteristics it had before the change. In order to truly "change one's clothes;" one must alter the characteristics of the clothing itself, and not merely *exchange* one unaltered piece of clothing for another unaltered piece of clothing. Normally "changing one's clothes" makes no changes whatsoever in the clothing itself; but rather only changes what one is wearing.

And the key here; is that one can *exchange* only with that which is available. One cannot exchange what one is wearing, with clothing they do not have available to them.

So the better translation would be: "their women did *exchange* the natural use into that which is against nature."

The original Greek word translated as both "*natural*" and "*nature*" is:

> "5446 phusikŏs; from 5449; "*physical*", i.e. (by impl.) *instinctive*: - natural."[2.40]

The original Greek word translated as "use" is:

> "5540 chrēsis; from 5530; *employment*, i.e. (spec.) sexual *intercourse* (as an occupation of the body): - use's."[2.41]

The original Greek word translated as "against" is:

> "3844 para; a prim. prep.; prop. *near*, i.e. (with gen.) *from*, *beside* (lit. or fig.), (with dat.) *at* (or *in*) the *vicinity* of (obj. or subj.), (with acc.) to the *proximity* with (local [espec. *beyond* or *opposed* to] or causal [*on account* of])..."[2.42]

Para is translated only twice as "*against*" in the entire New Testament; here and in Romans 4:18.[2.43]

There are over eighteen different Greek words translated as "against" in the New Testament.[2.44]

The most common Greek word translated as "against" in the New Testament, appearing fifty seven times[2.45] is:

> "2596 kata; a prim. particle; (prep.) *down* (in place or time), in varied relations (according to the case [gen., dat. or acc.] with which it is joined)..."[2.46]

The next most common Greek word translated as "against" in the New Testament, appearing thirty six times,[2.47] is:

> "1909 ĕpi; a prim. prep. prop. mean. *superimposition* (of time, place, order, etc.), as a relation of *distribution* [with the gen.], i.e. *over, upon,* etc.; of *rest* (with the dat.] *at, on,* etc.; of *direction* (with the acc.) *towards, upon,* etc...."[2.48]

These other Greek words are addressed here, in order to show that: "*against nature*," seems to be a very misleading translation. A better and *literal* translation of *para phusikŏs*; would be: "next to the physical." The use of "*against*" probably meant "next to" at that time; as in: "lean it against the wall;" rather than "in opposition to."

And the phrase "into that which is" is actually two Greek words.

The *first* original Greek word is:

> "1519 ĕis; a prim. prep.; to or into (indicating the point reached or entered), of place, time, or (fig.) purpose (result, etc.); also in adv. phrases..."[2.49]

And the *second* appears to be the Greek την, which appears to simply mean "the."[2.50]

So this statement would literally read: "their women did exchange, (*mĕtallassō*); the physical, (*phusikŏs*); sexual intercourse (*chrēsis*); to that which is next to, (*para*); *the physical*, (*phusikŏs*).

What is it that is "next to the physical," or *para phusikŏs*? By Hobson's choice; "things" that are in some way or manner *not physical*, of course.

Although *paranormal* will be addressed in great detail later in this work, a distinction should be made here. *Paraphusikŏs*, (presented here as one word); and *paranormal* are *similar*, but are not *synonyms*.

Paranormal refers to that which is next to the "norm;" with *norm* here referring to the "right angle"
intersection of body and soul; i.e.; *physical* life. Here the *immaterial* is symbolized by the *vertical*; and the *material* symbolized by the *horizontal*. Thus there can be no *paranormal* without this *norm*; i.e.; unless and until something is *physically alive*.

Paraphusikŏs refers to that which is next to the *physical* or *matter*; i.e.; the *material* realm. What is it that is next to the material realm? Since the presence of matter is a binary—it is either present or it is not, irrespective of the *quantity*; some type of non-material, or *immaterial* realm is the only answer possible.

Given this, then what does: "their women did exchange, (*mĕtallassō*); the physical, (*phusikŏs*); sexual intercourse (*chrēsis*); to that which is next to, (*para*); *the physical*, (*phusikŏs*)" actually mean? This is asked with the understanding that again *paraphusikŏs* means some type of non-material realm?

What we are *not* told, is that this: "to that which is next to," the physical; was also physical, (*phusikŏs*). To state that the *physical*, is or was next to the *physical*; would seem to make little sense.

Meaning; the passage *does not read*, and thus *does not mean*: "their women did exchange, (*mĕtallassō*); the physical, (*phusikŏs*); sexual intercourse (*chrēsis*); to physical, (*phusikŏs*); sexual intercourse (*chrēsis*); with that which is next to, (*para*); *the physical*, (*phusikŏs*)." Thus this does not refer to physical sexual intercourse with non-physical entities.

The most likely meaning; is that their women did exchange, (*mĕtallassō*); the physical, (*phusikŏs*); sexual intercourse (*chrēsis*); *to be in accord with* that which is next to, (*para*); *the physical*, (*phusikŏs*).

And since prior to this, they were in accord with *God*; as Romans 1:21 begins with: "*Because that, when they knew God;*" this exchange was to here be in accord with something next to the physical, or something *immaterial*; but here it was now no longer God. This likely refers to the *neither* or *nether* world; and that which was banished to the same.

The remainder of the translation of these passages: "*men leaving the natural use of the woman, burned in their lust one toward another; men with men working that which is unseemly;*" appears to mean what it appears to state. Thus these passages most likely refer to homosexual activities.

But it seems that there was a price to be paid, as we are then told at the end of Romans 1:27, and continuing on in verse 28: "*and receiving in themselves that recompence of their error which was meet. And even as they did not like to retain God in their knowledge, God gave them over to a reprobate mind, to do those things which are not convenient.*"

The actual Greek word translated as "recompence" is:

> "489 antimisthia; from a comp. of *473* and *3408*; *requital, correspondence*: - recompense."[2.51]

The actual Greek word translated as "error" is:

> "4106 planē; fem. of *4108* (as abstr.); obj. *fraudulence*; subj. a *straying* from orthodoxy or piety..."[2.52]

When we are told here: "*and receiving in themselves that recompence of their error which was meet;*" this sounds suspiciously like *karma*. They received just compensation for their "*error*," or *planē*. [It must be noted that *planē*, as will soon be seen, is quite similar to another Greek word: *planaō*. It was because of *planaō*, that Satan was ejected from the immaterial realm. See: "*Ostium Ab Inferno*"]

We are also told: "*God gave them over to a reprobate mind, to do those things which are not convenient.*"

The actual Greek word translated as "reprobate" is:

> "96 adŏkimŏs; from *1* (as a neg. particle) and *1384*; *unapproved* i.e. *rejected*; by impl. *worthless* (lit. or mor.)..."[2.53]

The actual Greek word translated as "mind" is:

> "3563 nŏus; prob. from the base of *1097*; the *intellect*, i.e. *mind* (divine or human; in thought, feeling or will); by impl. *meaning*: - mind, understanding. Comp. 5590"[2.54]

The actual Greek word translated as "convenient" is:

> "2520 kathēkō; from 2596 and 2240; to reach to, i.e. (neut. of pres. act. part., fig. as adj.) becoming: - convenient fit."[2.55]

Thus it seems that the: "*recompence of their error which was meet;*" was: "*a reprobate mind, to do those things which are not convenient.*"

What we are *not* told here is that they were killed or destroyed. And we are not told of anyone turning into a pillar of salt, for merely watching anything.

But it must be asked how much of this penalty or *karma*, was the direct consequence of the *homosexual* activities; and how much was because of all of the other "bad things" described.

Prior to engaging in what reasonably appears to be *certain* homosexual behavior; (Romans 1:27: ("*the men, leaving the natural use of the woman, burned in their lust one toward another; men with men*"); and *arguable* homosexual behavior, (Romans 1:24: ("*uncleanness through the lusts of their own hearts, to dishonour their own bodies between themselves*"); there were many "bad things" going on.

We are told in these verses that they had also: "*knew God, they glorified him not as God,*" and: "*became vain in their imaginations,*" and: "*their foolish heart was darkened,*" and: "*professing themselves to be wise, they became fools,*" and: "*changed the glory of the uncorruptible God into an image made like to corruptible man, and to birds, and fourfooted beasts, and creeping things,*" and: "*changed the truth of God into a lie,*" and: "*worshipped and served the creature more than the Creator.*"

But in order to accurately determine "how evil" homosexuality is in the eyes of God; one would need to be able to accurately apportion the penalty, or "*recompense*" provided, with regard to each of these evil acts. However, although there may be a plethora of *opinion*; there is no Biblical *evidence* available with which to do this.

If then strictly for the purpose of argument, it is assumed that God "gave them a pass" on each and every one of these evil behaviors *except* the homosexuality; a "worst case scenario" for the "evilness" of homosexuality could be established.

In furtherance of intellectual honesty, and continuity of thought; the passages that *immediately follow* Romans 1:26-28 are provided.

Romans 1:29-32 tells us:

"Being filled with all unrighteousness,
fornication, wickedness, covetousness,
maliciousness; full of envy, murder,
debate, deceit, malignity; whisperers,

Backbiters, haters of God, despiteful,
proud, boasters, inventors of evil things,
disobedient to parents,

Without understanding, covenantbreakers,
without natural affection,
implacable, unmerciful:

Who knowing the judgment of God,
that they which commit such things
are worthy of death,
not only do the same, but have
pleasure in them that do them."[2.56]

Why is Paul immediately providing this litany of bad behaviors; and what does this have to do with the likely homosexuality previously addressed? And what about the: "*they which commit such things are worthy of death;*" part?

Earlier we were told of *primary causation*: "*Because that, when they knew God, they glorified him not as God, neither were thankful; but became vain in their imaginations, and their foolish heart was darkened. Professing themselves to be wise, they became fools, And changed the glory of the uncorruptible God into an image made like to corruptible man, and to birds, and fourfooted beasts, and creeping things. Who changed the truth of God into a lie, and worshipped and served the creature more than the Creator, who is blessed for ever. Amen.*"

One *result* of this *primary* cause was: *Wherefore God also gave them up to uncleanness through the lusts of their own hearts, to dishonour their own bodies between themselves.*"

And then, because of these "*lusts*:" "*their women did change the natural use into that which is against nature*" and: "*men leaving the natural use of the woman, burned in their lust one toward another; men with men working that which is unseemly*."

It seems that there could be and were *other* types of results of this *primary*, (Romans 1:21-25), cause; instead of, or in addition to, these aforementioned "*lusts*," and likely resultant homosexuality from these same "*lusts*."

And it seems that it is these *other*, (non-homosexual), types of *results* of this primary *cause* contained in Romans 1:21-25, of which Paul is speaking here in Romans 1:29-32.

The reasonable read, is that the homosexuality issue was in a sense "resolved" when: "*and receiving in themselves that recompence of their error which was meet. And even as they did not like to retain God in their knowledge, God gave them over to a reprobate mind, to do those things which are not convenient.*"

But it is not known how much of this "resolution" was directly related to the homosexuality; and how much was related to all of the other "bad behaviors" described in Romans 1:21-25 that preceded the homosexuality. It seems likely, that the majority of the "*recompence*" was for these other Romans 1:21-25 "bad behaviors;" with little if any for the probable homosexuality *result* described in Romans 1:27.

However; with regard to these *other*, (non-homosexual), types of behaviors listed by Paul here in Romans 1:29-32; unlike the "*recompence*" for those in Romans 1:21-25; we are told: "*they which commit such things are worthy of death.*"

The actual Greek word translated here as "worthy" is:

> "514 axiŏs; prob. from *71*; *deserving*, *comparable* or *suitable* (as if *drawing* praise): - due, reward, meet, [un-] worthy."[2.57]

The actual Greek word translated here as "death" is:

> "2288 thanatŏs; from *2348*; (prop. an adj. used as a noun) *death* (lit. or fig.) : - x deadly, (be . . .) death."[2.58]

Thus it seems that with regard to all of these resultant behaviors listed by Paul in Romans 1:29-32, regarding which Paul tells us: "*they which commit such things are worthy of death.*"

However, it seems those resultant *sexual* behaviors described in Romans 1:26-28: "*their women did change the natural use into that which is against nature*" and: "*men leaving the natural use of the woman, burned in their lust one toward another; men with men working that which is unseemly;*" are not: *worthy of death.*".

Instead; these particular, (lusts, and subsequent homosexuality), behaviors' in Romans 1:26-28 are or were "worthy of;" or their "*recompence*" was: "*a reprobate mind, to do those things which are not convenient.*"

Thus even if it is assumed that this "*recompence*" was due entirely to homosexuality; which is highly unlikely; then it becomes clear that the homosexuality had a *lesser* penalty. And in addition; this assumption requires that the causative behaviors listed Romans 1:21-25, including the idolatry, had no penalty—and this is likely not so.

The next purported Biblical "reference" to homosexuality, appears chronologically in 1 Corinthians 6:9-11 (KJV):

"Know ye not that the unrighteous
shall not inherit the kingdom of God?
Be not deceived: neither fornicators,

nor idolaters, nor adulterers,
nor effeminate,
nor abusers of themselves with mankind,

Nor thieves, nor covetous, nor drunkards,
nor revilers, nor extortioners,
shall inherit the kingdom of God.

And such were some of you:
but ye are washed, but ye are sanctified,
but ye are justified in the name of the
Lord Jesus, and by the Spirit of our God."[2.59]

At first it seems the key word, and perhaps the only word, in these passages linking them in any way to homosexuality, would be the word "*effeminate.*" Or could it instead be the: "*abusers of themselves with mankind*" part?

The actual Greek word translated as "effeminate" is:

> "3120 malakŏs; of uncert. affin.; *soft*, i.e. *fine* (clothing); fig. a *catamite*: - effeminate, soft."[2.60]

According to Strong, verse 9 is the only time the word *effeminate* appears as a *translation* in the entire KJV Bible.[2.61]

It is unclear how "*effeminate*" relates to homosexuality. This may be *stereotypically* accurate; but clearly in no way represents an accurate means to determine sexual "orientation"—assuming of course one cares, and it is any of their business.

The literal definition of *malakŏs* simply means: "*soft*, i.e. *fine* (clothing)." Thus there seems to be no reason to group one who is *malakŏs* or "soft;" with "*thieves*," "*drunkards*," and "*extortioners*."

The *figurative* meaning of *malakŏs* is a "*catamite*." A *catamite* is a pubescent boy who is "kept" for sexual purposes by what today would be called a *pedophile*. But the more accurate and specific term for the man is *pederast*; and *pederasty* collectively refers to a *man* and a young *boy*.

But *catamite* refers to the pubescent boy, and not the adult. Likely this boy either did not yet have, or just had his Bar Mitzvah. Thus although the Bar Mitzvah technically makes the boy responsible for his actions, it seems odd to include him in these grouping. In Western culture, a thirteen year old boy, Bar Mitzvah or not, is not considered to have "enough on board" to consent to this type of a relationship.

Perhaps the purported reference to homosexuality, is the: "*abusers of themselves with mankind*" part.

The original Greek word translated as "*abusers of themselves with mankind*" is:

> "733 arsĕnŏkŏitēs; from 730 and 2845; a *sodomite*: - abuser of (that defile) self with mankind."[2.62]

> "730 arrhēn; or arsēn; prob. from *142*; *male* (as stronger for *lifting*): - male, man."[2.63]

> "2845 kŏitē; from *2749*; a *couch*; by extens. *cohabitation*; by impl. the male *sperm*: - bed, chambering, x conceive."[2.64]

So here we have it. *Arsĕnŏkŏitēs* is a "Sodomite;" and is translated here as: "*abusers of themselves with mankind.*" The problem with this of course, is that again; in the "Sodom" passages that are generally, (but erroneously), considered as relating to *homosexuality*; it seems the only one clearly mentioning anything having to do with any type of *sexual* activity was Lot—and it also seems he offered two *females* to a group of purported homosexual *males*.

Perhaps Paul was unaware of the *lack* of any clear references to homosexuality in these Genesis passages relating to Sodom; and thus here he in fact meant *arsĕnŏkŏitēs* to refer to homosexuals. If so; then why did he also include another indirect reference, *malakŏs*, translated as "*effeminate*;" but *literally* meaning only "soft;" and only *figuratively* meaning the aforementioned "catamite?"

Or instead; perhaps here *arsĕnŏkŏitēs*, defined as "Sodomite;" refers to *all* of the behaviors; i.e.; their behaviors *in-toto*; of those in Sodom which God had previously described as: "*their sin is very grievous*." But it remains unclear how a "man" and or a "couch," (arrhēn; or arsēn; prob. from *142*;

male" + "kŏitē; from 2749; a *couch*"); would suffice in this regard. In fact, this could also be used as a euphemism for a *psychiatrist*.

If Paul understood that homosexuality had little or nothing to do with God's destruction of Sodom; then his inclusion of homosexuality via the *figurative* meaning of *malakŏs*, here meaning a *catamite*; would make some degree of sense—if he were in fact trying to include homosexuality behavior itself in this group.

However the better argument for this would be that it was the aforementioned *pederast*, today referred to with the more general term *pedophilia*; that was the actual offense he was trying to include. This of course represents more than mere homosexuality. In Western culture, this would represent serious felonious behavior, and is punishable by a serious prison term.

The final purported Biblical reference to homosexuality, appears chronologically in 1 Timothy 1:10-11 (KJV):

"For whoremongers, for them that defile themselves with mankind,
for menstealers, for liars, for perjured persons, and if there be any other thing that is contrary to sound doctrine;

According to the glorious gospel of the blessed God,
which was committed to my trust."[2.65]

At first blush, it is difficult to determine what is going on here; and precisely which term(s) in these passages it is that purportedly refer(s) to homosexuality.

The passages that immediately precede the above 1 Timothy 1:10-11, (1 Timothy 1:8-9), provide the context.

1 Timothy 1:8-9 (KJV) tells us:

"*But we know that the law is good,*
if a man use it lawfully;

Knowing this,that the law is not made
for a righteous man,
but for the lawless and disobedient,
for the ungodly and for sinners,
for unholy and profane,
for murderers of fathers and murderers
of mothers, for manslayers,"[2.66]

In fact; 1 Timothy 1:9 above, ends not with a period; but rather ends with a comma. So the purpose of these passages taken together, (1 Timothy 8:8-11, *in-toto*); is to discuss the purpose of "law;" with a litany of those for whom the law is necessary; and then with a possible reference to homosexuality in verse 10, with the "catch all" of: "*and if there be any other thing that is contrary to sound doctrine.*"

But it seems that: "*them that defile themselves with mankind,*" represents the most likely candidate for the purported reference to homosexuality.

Once again, the actual Greek word, but here translated as "*that defile;*" and not the previous translation as "*abuser,*" is again: "733 arsĕnŏkŏitēs; from 730 and 2845; a *sodomite*: - abuser of (that defile) self with mankind."[2.67]

But to defile, generally means to make impure—and here: "*with mankind.*" It seems reasonable that any and all of those others mentioned in Timothy: "*whoremongers,*" "*menstealers,*" "*liars,*" "*perjured persons,*" "*ungodly,*" "*sinners,*" "*unholy and profane,*" "*murderers of fathers,*" and "*murderers of mothers,*" and "*manslayers;*" also represent: "*them that defile themselves with mankind.*" Thus the translation seems to be much more broad.

So if this actual translation of *arsĕnŏkŏitēs* as "*that defile*" ("*themselves with mankind*"); represents a euphemism for homosexual; but although utilized euphemistically, is nevertheless provided in order to *distinguish* homosexuality, from those other specific types of actions in this litany provided in Timothy. It has already been reasonably established that homosexuality is against God's will; but the "*recompence*" is a much lesser penalty than: "*worthy of death.*" And again, this assumes that all of the other wicked behavior received a "pass."

If so; why then is there this *distinction* and *difference*? The answer; is that if it is homosexuality and homosexuality *alone*; there then seems to be no *victim* readily available. Most of these other actions listed require a nonconsenting victim; with perhaps only "*ungodly,*" and "*unholy and profane,*" not requiring an *immediate* victim—depending upon precisely what subsequent *actions* are undertaken because of these "*ungodly,*" and "*unholy and profane,*" *conditions* or *states.*

This would not be so with *malakŏs* translated as "*effeminate;*" if actually meaning *catamite*; as this requires a *victim*; either *unwilling*, or *incapable* of "informed consent" because of age. Thus this could in no way qualify as: "homosexuality and homosexuality *alone.*"

In conclusion, it seems that there is little or no Biblical justification for that which is purported to be "Biblically" so regarding homosexuality.

The "lynchpin" for these purported but erroneous "views;" is the general belief about the *reasons* for the destruction of Sodom as contained in Genesis 19:1-5. But an unbiased read of these passages, reasonably proves that these passages in fact actually have little or nothing to do with homosexuality.

This purported relationship to homosexuality; is largely based upon the *mistranslation* of the first appearance of *yâda'* translated *euphemistically* as: "sexual relations;" and not translated *literally*: "to know."

It is likely that those speaking for the crowd were in fact lying; but they were lying about their true intentions regarding the *literal* definition of *yâda'*; and not proffering the *euphemism* for *yâda'*—as Lot himself did when offering two *females* to *men*; who we are nevertheless supposed to believe were *homosexuals*. This is not to say that there was not homosexuality in Sodom; but rather that homosexuality was not any significant part of this particular "story."

The references in Leviticus 18:22 and 20:13 are concerned only with personal views of homosexuality.

The references in Mark 10:6-9 are concerned with *divorce*, and seem to have nothing whatsoever to do with homosexuality.

Romans 1:26-28 in fact do seem to clearly relate to homosexuality; and we are told the *process* by which this happened. And it is clear in these passages that homosexuality is considered therein as sinful behavior.

However when examining these passages in Romans in *context*, it becomes clear that homosexuality; unlike the other behaviors listed; requires or required a penalty different than the penalty for those sinful behaviors in the litany which follows. Specifically; homosexuality at most required: "*recompence of their error which was meet*;" with the same being: "*a reprobate mind, to do those things which are not convenient*." And it is not known how much of a factor the actual homosexuality itself was in determining this penalty, given all else that went on which ultimately led to this. But with regard to the other types of sinful behaviors listed, we are told: "*they which commit such things are worthy of death*."

It is in 1 Corinthians 6:9-11 where *malakŏs*, translated as: "*effeminate*" appears. But *if* the true meaning here is "*catamite*," this would make some degree of sense for its inclusion. The one who kept the *catamite* is a *pederast*, which today is referred to with the more general term *pedophile*—which today is a serious *criminal* offense in most civilized areas.

It must be asked how much less of a sin it would be if a "catamite" were of the opposite gender of the "pederast;" or today the *pedophile*. Meaning; that the pubescent child "kept" was *female*; but the pedophile was *male*; or the reverse. However less disgusting it is that one may find this "arrangement;" this "reduction in disgust," would then necessarily reveal the actual true level of sinfulness of the actual homosexual component—at least to that particular person.

1 Timothy 1:10-11; and that which immediately precedes it, is largely about "*the law*;" and at best only tangentially relates to homosexuality. This seems to be an affirmation that homosexuality is considered as sinful; but much less so than other listed "sins," as there is no victim or harm to another; *as long as there is consent* between two, (non-catamite), adults; and thus homosexuality is all there is that is involved.

It is often said by many, that: "God hates homosexuality, but He loves homosexuals." It is unclear Biblically, where either of these statements is to be found. Particularly given the fact that as previously stated; according to Strong; no translation as "homosexual," or "homosexuality," appears anywhere in the entire KJV Bible.

It seems that over the millennia there has been both tremendous hatred of homosexuality; as well as persecution of homosexuals. Often this is based upon those claiming to be doing: "The Lord's Work." Perhaps these are privy to information that God did not see fit to tell anyone else; or perhaps not.

And the Biblical *mistranslations*, most especially those *mistranslations* pertaining to the events surrounding *Sodom*; fuel this. After all, if homosexuality were such sinful behavior as to justify what God did with Sodom, then it must really be bad—Right? The answer is no He didn't, no it isn't, and this "really be bad" statement is wrong—at least according to what His word reasonably states. To put this in "Catholic terms;" at least Biblically, homosexuality alone would be considered no more than a "venial sin."

The key to understanding the hatred of homosexuality and homosexuals; lies in the previously referenced passages in Leviticus; regarding what reasonably appears to be homosexuality. Here the word translated as "abomination" in each of these verses again is: "8441 tôw'êbâh; or tô'êbâh; fem. act. part. of 8581 prop. something *disgusting* (mor.), i.e. (as noun) an *abhorrence*; espec. *idolatry* or (concr.) an *idol*."

Thus here homosexuality is: "something disgusting," to the writers; just as it may be to many others even today—whether admitted or not. But whether or not one finds homosexuality to be: "something disgusting," is not the issue. Many people often find much of that which others do as "something disgusting," *to them*; e.g.; "Steak Tartare." The issue is not what *their* eyes see, or a matter of *taste*; but rather what *His* eyes see, and the mater of *evil*, and or *wicked*.

So when: "I don't like it." is combined with: "And He don't like it either, look at what he did to them at Sodom;" the result is predictable, and unfortunately a matter of history.

Is homosexuality *evil*; with *evil* here meaning against the will of God? It seems that the answer is yes, if a fair read of His word is the reference. This is why it is sinful—albeit a minor one.

Is homosexuality *wicked*; with *wicked* here meaning causing harm to others? If it is just homosexuality alone, it seems that the answer is no, if a fair read of His word is the reference.

How can something be evil, but not wicked; or wicked but not evil? The answer to this is contained in the definitions. The Crucifixion was *wicked*, but not *evil* by these definitions. Had the devil succeeded at Gethsemane, and Jesus not "gone through with it;" this would have been *evil*, but avoided the *wickedness* of the act. But that was one of the very reasons Jesus had walked the earth.

Here is seems that homosexuality alone, is evil; but is not wicked. Why is it evil? Because it causes one to miss some particular mark, and not share in the prize—as is the case with all sin.

The two most common words translated as "sin" in the New Testament[2.68] are:

> "266 hamartia; from 264; sin (prop. abstr.): - offence, sin (-ful)."[2.69]

and

> "264 hamartano, perh. from 1 (as a neg. particle) and the base of 3313; prop. to miss the mark (and so not share in the prize), i.e. (fig.) to err, esp. (mor.) to sin; - for your faults, offend, sin, trespass."[2.70]

It is primarily the *mistranslation* of one word in Genesis, that has caused so much misery, for so many, for so long—even by those who were trying to, and may have actually believed, they were doing the will of God.

This was quite clever on the part of the enemy, both as a direct attack on children of God who are homosexual; and an indirect attack on those children of God who are not. But this was only one part of his plan.

3

The True Gay

What is the "true gay?"

Or perhaps the better question would be: "Precisely what *actuality* is or was it that the word 'gay' symbolized; prior to the somewhat recent inclusion of, or supplanting by, sexual matters?"

Often in *common* usages, the word "gay" used to be considered as synonymous with "happiness," or "joy;" and there are in fact some commonalities. However, as will be seen; "gay," here meaning the "true gay," has characteristics well beyond these particular subjective "states."

Some terms will be defined here, but solely for the purpose of this analysis. Others may proffer different definitions for different purposes. And as will also be seen, it is difficult to obtain precise meanings—even when the "etymology" is thoroughly researched.

Happiness is largely a positive emotional *result* of something that has *happened.* First the pleasurable event occurs; and *then* there is happiness. Happiness is generally the *subjective* result of some *objective* cause. Happiness is *short* term, and *tactical* in nature. Thus happiness can and will dissipate over time; and can also easily be supplanted by other events; i.e.; "conditions on the ground."

One can envision a "number line" with regard to happiness:

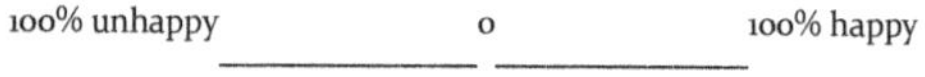

100% unhappy ____________ 0 ____________ 100% happy

A distinction must be made here regarding the use of the term: "unhappy." Here with the use of this diagram, it is stipulated that "100% unhappy" is not the mere absence of "happy;" but also the 100% presence of that which is commonly referred to as "sad." Thus the *center* of this diagram would then indicate the *absence* of either "happy" or "sad;" i.e.; "I am neither happy nor sad."

This could have been done differently, with "100% unhappy" meaning the absence of happiness, and also the absence of "sad." Had this been done, then the *left side* of this diagram would have then indicated the *absence* of either "happy" or "sad;" i.e.; "I am neither happy nor sad."

Likely neither ends of this "number line," as stipulated; are ever actually reached—despite the fact that one may believe so. Depending upon *events*; i.e.; that which *happens*; the location moves left or right from wherever we "were;" to wherever events "take us," in the *happiness* or *unhappiness*, (here sad), "department."

There is no memory involved in happiness; except perhaps for intellectual *recollections* of previous states of happiness. Although the quest for happiness may be a *causative* factor in *hope*, (roughly: *desire* plus *expectation*), with regard to *future* events; happiness itself is not hope, and does not itself contain hope.

And although *hope* includes *expectation*, the level of *confidence* in this "hoped for" expectation actually *manifesting*, can vary greatly.

When the levels of confidence in the manifestation of this expectation approach 100%; to this same extent, a *similarity* to *joy* begins. However *hope* is much more *specific* with respect to a particular event, than is *joy*.

Perhaps better stated: *Hope* is much more concerned with the occurrence of *a specific* "happiness causing" event. *Joy* is concerned with the occurrence of *some* "happiness causing" event—irrespective of what that particular event will in fact be.

A child *hoping* for a bicycle for her birthday; along with a reasonably high degree of confidence that this will happen; represents *hope*. Were it the case that this same child hoping with the same level of confidence for *any* "happiness causing" birthday gift, this would be *similar* to *joy*, but is not actually *joy*, because although the confidence may substantial; it is likely not close to, or at 100%.

In the case of *joy*, it is not a level of *confidence* that some "happiness causing" event will happen; but rather essentially *knowing* that some type of "happiness causing" event will in fact happen—even if precisely *what* or precisely *when* remains unknown.

How does one "know" this? The answer is *faith*; but not in any way faith in the usual proffered "religious" sense.

In fact, the most common word translated as "faith" in the KJV New Testament[3.1] is actually:

> "4102 pistis; from *3982*; *persuasion*, i.e. *credence*; mor. *conviction* (of *religious* truth, or the truthfulness of God or a religious teacher), espec. *reliance* upon Christ for salvation; abstr. *constancy* in such profession; by extens. the system of religious (Gospel) *truth* itself: - assurance, belief, believe, faith, fidelity."[3.2]

> "3982 pěithō; a prim. verb; to *convince* (by argument, true or false); by anal. to *pacify* or *conciliate* (by other fair means); reflex. or pass. to *assent* (to evidence or authority), to *rely* (by inward certainty): - agree, assure, believe, have confidence, be (wax) [(?

> unreadable)], make friend, obey, persuade, trust, yield."[3.3]

As can be seen, the most common New Testament word translated as "faith," is in no way related to "blind faith;" but rather is achieved by: "*persuasion*," and: "to *convince* (by argument, true or false)."

Thus that aforementioned child *hoping* for a bicycle for her birthday; along with a reasonably high degree of *confidence* that this will happen, here representing *hope*; was likely based upon her previous experiences. She was *persuaded* and *convinced* to some extent that her parents would do this; but not persuaded and convinced completely. There was a reasonable level of confidence (*con*, with; and *fidelis* faith); but she did not effectively *know*.

The same can be said, if it were the case that this same child, hoping with the same level of confidence for *any* "happiness causing" birthday gift. This was so because she had previously been *persuaded* and *convinced*, and this would be *similar* to *joy*; but is not *joy*, because she did not actually *know*.

If and when there is *no reasonable doubt* that *some* type of "happiness causing" birthday gift will manifest; because there had been *pistis*, or "*persuasion*," and "to *convince* (by argument, true or false);" say because of her parents previous actions, this would be *joy*.

Since in the long run, the *solipsists* may have a valid point; reasonably *knowing* "a thing" to be so, as opposed to merely *believing* a thing to be so, reasonably requires two things:

The first is a reasonable *threshold*, for making the decision that a thing is what it purports to be, (it is an *actuality*).

The second is the presence of *evidence* that is sufficient to *meet* or *exceed* this threshold.

The first is *subjective*, and often emotions play into the establishment of this threshold.

But one would think that the second, *evidence*; would be *objective*. However there are some, who for whatever reason(s), will never believe that man landed on the moon—no matter what level of evidence is presented to them. And others will believe it is actually the face of Jesus in that pancake—because it looks that way to them—even though only to them.

To the reasonable person that *knows*; their *reality* is such that it is a *certainty*, that whatever it is; is an *actuality*. Thus whatever *attributes* this actuality is known to also have, can likewise be considered *actualities*. If it is reasonably known that "the set" exists; then all of the "subsets" likewise necessarily, (cannot reasonably not), exist.

It matters little that others may refer to this "knowledge" as: "that's just what they believe they know;" simply because these others have either decided upon a different *threshold*, or have not: "seen the evidence." But to the person that "knows;" they "know they know," and thus act accordingly.

Prior to election night 2016, most of the readers of: "*Donald Trump Candidacy According to*

Matthew," had previously made the determination that the evidence they had seen therein was true; and was in fact applicable to Donald Trump. They therefore then *knew* that no matter how it may *appear*, Donald Trump was going to win the presidency—and this was months before he was even nominated. So to these; it was never a matter of *if*, but only a matter of *when* this actuality would manifest. Thus to these; on election night 2016, it was never a matter of *what* would be declared that evening, but only a matter of *when*. This was based upon *knowledge*, and not desire.

This is not provided here to in any way suggest that all who "knew" the inevitable outcome were *joyful*; as this clearly would not be so. The truth is that roughly half of the country voted for Trump's opponent. Rather this is provided only to illustrate and distinguish the "know" part of joy; as opposed to merely "believe." Those who understood the Biblical "kingdom of heaven" principles; and would admit that there was no rational explanation other than these applied to Trump at that time; knew he would win—whether *happy* about it or not.

Happiness and joy are *subjective* states. However; each of these states can produce *objective* changes in appearance. Both *happy* and *joyful* persons can often appear as such, although distinguishing which it is can be difficult. One state of *objective* physical appearance due to either *happiness* or *joy*; could be best described as *gladness*.

According to Chambers, "glad" is derived from:

> "*adj*. Probably before 1200 *glad* joyful, merry, mild, gracious, pleased, in Layamon's *Chronicle of Britian*; developed from Old Engish *glæd* bright, shining, joyous, glad (about 725, in *Beowulf*); cognate with Old Frisian *gled* smooth, Old Saxon *glad-* (in compounds such as *gladmōdi* joyous, happy)..."[3.4]

This state of being *glad*, or *gladness*, as per the original: "*glæd* bright, shining;" is visible to anyone who looks. It is a *physical* or *objective* result, of an *emotional* or *subjective* condition. How this person looks to others on the *outside*, is the result of what is happening on the *inside*.

The level of the resultant *gladness*, or: "bright, shining," ("developed from Old Engish *glæd* bright, shining,") is proportional to the *stimulus* or the *cause*. *Happiness* can produce a certain level of gladness, but generally *after* the fact. *Joy* is capable of producing a much greater level of gladness; i.e.; brighter and shinier; and generally is *before* the fact.

The aforementioned young "birthday girl;" is now pirouetting around the living room on the morning of her birthday; because she: "knows it is going to be good"—even though she has no idea what "it" is. This cause is *joy*, and the resultant *gladness*, is visible to all.

And the reason she *knows*, is because she has been *persuaded* and *convinced* by previous events.

Thus she has *faith*, or *pistis*; and this produces the *joy*—at least when birthday time comes around.

But this *gladness* is limited to that for which there is *faith* or *pistis*— and only for that which the girl likes; i.e.; "is fun." Later that day, when her aunt arrives with a birthday present for her, there may be *politeness*; but the *gladness* disappears. This is because the girl has *faith* or *pistis* that "Auntie," will give her something "un-fun." She has been *persuaded* and *convinced* of this, because of past experiences. Or stated another way; there is no *faith* or *pistis*, that a "fun thing" will manifest.

And this *gladness* is also limited to that which is *within* this girl. The source of this gladness is within, even though this gladness can have some effect on others—"like a breath of fresh air."

When the *source* of what appears to be *gladness* is not from *within*, and thus *limited*; but rather the *source* is from *without*, and thus *unlimited*; this is *gay*. *Gay* is similar in appearance to *gladness*, but has an entirely different immediate source.

Chambers indicates the etymology of the word "gay" is:

> "*adj*. Probably about 1300, splendid or beautiful; earlier, as a surname (1178); borrowed from Old French *gai* gay, merry; perhaps from Frankish (compare Old High German *gāhi* rapid, impetuous, modern German *jäh* hasty, sudden). The meaning of joyous or merry appeared probably about 1380. The slang sense of homosexual is

> first recorded in 1951, apparently shortened from an earlier compound gay cat homosexual boy (about 1935, in underworld and prison slang), but used earlier for a young tramp or hobo, often one attached to an older tramp and usually with a connotation of homosexuality (1897, in American English slang). —n. a homosexual. 1971, American English..."[3.5]

As can easily be seen, there are again differences in opinion as to precisely when and how "gay" obtained its "modern" meaning. It must also be noted that the term "cat" included therein; is likely a shortened form of *catamite*, which was addressed in the previous chapter. The inclusion of "gay" here as an adjective; is likely the result of the belief that "cat," is slang with *feline* origins; rather than a truncation of another word, where the use of this particular adjective would not be necessary.

The above definition first states "splendid or beautiful." "Splendid" is a word not usually understood today, as it is often used merely as an affirmation of a high degree of acceptability. However splendid is actually derived from the Latin infinitive *splendere*, meaning "be bright, shine."[3.6]

Thus the first word in the definition of gay, *splendid*; actually means to be bright and shiny; and the second word arguably implies that the "beautiful," is because of the brightness and shine;

and not for other reasons, such as other *physical* attributes.

Gladness was previously defined as "bright, shining." Here *gay* is similarly defined. What is the difference? With *gladness*, the "bright, shining" is caused by and thus is a *reflection* of that which is *within*, and as stated, is thus limited to that which is within.

But with regard to *gay*, the bright and shining is the result of that which is *without*; and thus is not limited by that which is within—except for "cooperation" with that which is without.

Gladness is similar to a *reflector*; but *gay* is similar to a *lamp*.

According to Strong, the translation of any word as "gay," appears only once in the entire KJV Bible.[3.7]

This original Greek word translated once as "gay" is:

> "2985 lampas; from 2989; a "*lamp*" or *flambeau*: - lamp, light, torch."[3.8]

> "2989 lampō a prim. verb; to *beam*, i.e. *radiate* brilliancy (lit. or fig): - give light, shine."[3.9]

As can be seen, despite Strong listing *lampas* as being translated once as "*gay*;" *gay* is not listed as a translation; (the words after the : -); anywhere above.

The passage where this translation of *lampas* as "gay," is James 2:3 (KJV):

"And ye have respect to him that weareth the gay clothing, and say unto him, Sit thou here in a good place; and say to the poor, Stand thou there, or sit here under my footstool:"[3.10]

It is *lampas*, the *noun* that is translated as *gay* in this passage.[3.11] However; despite *lampas* being a noun, it is actually used as an *adjective* here to describe "*clothing*."

There is a relationship between *lampas* as a noun meaning: "*lamp* or *flambeau*," and translated as: "lamp, light, torch," (despite *gay* nevertheless being used here as an *adjective* to describe clothing);" and its purported root *lampō*, as a *verb* meaning: "to *beam*, i.e. *radiate* brilliancy (lit. or fig);" and *translated* as: "give light, shine."

All *lampas*, or *lamps* as commonly defined; are such because they: *lampō*, or: "*beam*, i.e. *radiate* brilliancy." But not all that: *lampō*, or "*beam*, i.e. *radiate* brilliancy," are *lampas*, or *lamps* as commonly defined. Stated another way: "All *lamps*, "*beam*," and "*radiate* brilliancy;" but not all things that "*beam*," and "*radiate* brilliancy;" are necessarily *lamps*, as *commonly* defined.

Ephesians 5:8-9 (KJV) tells us:

"For ye were sometimes darkness,
but now are ye light in the Lord:
walk as children of light:
(For the fruit of the Spirit is in all goodness

and righteousness and truth;)"[3.12]

Examination of the second verse, (verse 9), is "illuminating." Here in the *second* verse in Ephesians, (verse 9); the actual Greek word translated as "Spirit" is the verb *lampō*,[3.13] or again: "to *beam*, i.e. *radiate* brilliancy (lit. or fig): - give light, shine." The original word is *not* the noun *lampas*.

This translation of *lampō* here as "*Spirit*," represents a change. Prior to this, *lampō* was translated here as "*light*."[3.14] But it again must be remembered that *lampō* is a *verb*, and not a *noun*. Thus this "light" is action; and is not a person, place, or thing, such as "Spirit."

And we are told something about the "*fruit*" of this *lampō*; with the same being that it: "*is in all goodness and righteousness and truth*."

The inclusion of the word "*all*," makes this "all inclusive." Meaning; that *if* it is: "*goodness and righteousness and truth*;" *then* it is *required* that these contain this "*fruit*" of this *lampō*, in some way or manner.

The word "*for*" at the beginning of this passage, verse 9, can reasonably be replaced with "because." Therefore we are told: *because* "*the fruit*" of this *lampō*, "*is in all goodness and righteousness and truth*." Thus it is that which is contained in the *previous* verse, (verse 8); for which we are given this *reason* contained here in verse 9.

And verse 8 tells us: "*For ye were sometimes darkness, but now are ye light in the Lord: walk as children of light.*"

It must be noted that the word translated as "*sometimes*," is a bit tricky. As written, this implies that there was a period of time in the past when "*sometimes*" one *was*, (not *was in*), "*darkness*;" and "*sometimes*" one was not. Meaning; that in the past, being "*darkness*," (not being *in* darkness), itself was the *intermittent* state, that one went: "in and out of."

But the actual word translated here as "sometimes" is:

> "4218 pŏtĕ; from the base of 4225 and 5037; indef. adv., at *some time, ever*: - afore- (any, some-) time (s), at length (the last), (+ n-) ever, in the old time, in time past, once, when."[3.15]

Thus the passage would better read: "*For ye were* (at some time in the past) *darkness, but now are ye light in the Lord: walk as children of light.*"

It must again be noted that we are *not* told that we were *in* the darkness, and are now *in* the light. Rather we are told that we *were* darkness; and now we *are* light.

The word "light" appears twice here in verse 8: "*now are ye light in the Lord: walk as children of light.*"

But here this actual Geek word in verse 8, is neither *lampō*, nor *lampas*; but rather is:

> "5457 phōs; from an obsol. phaō (to *shine* or make *manifest*, espec. by *rays*;

> comp. *5316, 5346*); *luminousness* (in the widest application, nat. or artificial, abstr. or concr., lit. or fig.): - fire, light."[3.16]

> "5316 phainō; prol. for the base of *5457*; to *lighten* (*shine*), i.e. *show* (trans. or intrans., lit. or fig.)..."[3.17]

> "5346 phēmi; prop. the same as the base of *5457* and *5316*; to *show* or *make known* one's thoughts, i.e. *speak* or *say*..."[3.18]

The original Greek word translated as "darkness" is:

> "4655 skŏtŏs; from the base of *4639*; *shadiness*, i.e. *obscurity* (lit. or fig.): - darkness."[3.19]

Thus this "*darkness*," is actually due to *skŏtŏs*; or "*shadiness*, i.e. *obscurity*;" and is not any type of "*darkness*" due to lack of *lampō*; or that which is known to: "*beam*, i.e. *radiate* brilliancy (lit. or fig): - give light, shine." The "*fruit*" of this *lampō*, "*is in all goodness and righteousness and truth*."

This "*darkness*," or *skŏtŏs*, ended not when the *lampō* was "turned on;" as it was "on" all along. This "*darkness*," or *skŏtŏs*, ended when the "shade" was removed, and the *lampō*; or *beaming* or *radiation of brilliance*; was no longer "obscured."

And the result was *phōs*, translated as "*light*" meaning "to *shine* or make *manifest*, espec. by *rays*."

There is a difference between *lampō*, or the actual *source*, (*lampas*), of the "*beam*" or "radiate brilliancy;" and *phōs* as the actual *result*; or the shining or manifestation once the "shade" was removed.

It is this particular verb *lampō*, (now translated as the noun "Spirit"); whose "*fruit:*" "*is in all goodness and righteousness and truth.*" Thus it is that the *actions* of this verb *lampō* as a *cause*, that are providing that which is necessary for the *phōs* as the actual *result*; or the shining or manifestation, once the "shade" was removed

And we are then told to: "*walk as children of light.*"

Here the actual word translated as "walk" is:

> 4043 pĕripatĕō; from *4012* and *3961*; to *tread* all *around*, i.e. *walk* at large (espec. as proof of ability); fig. to *live deport oneself, follow* (as a companion or votary): - go, be occupied with, walk (about)."[3.20]

The word "votary" is not often seen today. Chambers provides the etymology of *votary*:

> "*n*. person devoted to something, devotee. 1546, person bound by vows to a religious life; formed in English

> from Latin *vōtum* VOW + English -*ary*..."[3.21]

Thus it seems clear that the translation of *pěripatěō* as "walk," refers to many or all of one's *behaviors*; and not merely the common meaning of ambulation.

The original Greek word translated as "children" is:

> "5043 těknŏn; from the base of 5088; a *child* (as *produced*): - child, daughter, son."[3.22]

Matthew 17:1-3 (KJV) tells us:

> "*And after six days Jesus taketh Peter,*
> *James, and John his brother,*
> *and bringeth them up into*
> *an high mountain apart,*
>
> *And was transfigured before them:*
> *and his face did shine as the sun,*
> *and his raiment was white as the light.*
>
> *And, behold, there appeared unto*
> *them Moses and Elias talking with him.*"[3.23]

The actual Greek word translated here as "*did shine,*" ("*as the sun*"); is the aforementioned: "2989 lampō a prim. verb; to *beam*, i.e. *radiate* brilliancy (lit. or fig): - give light, shine."[3.24]

The actual Greek word translated here as "light" in: "*his raiment was white as the light*," is the aforementioned: "5457 phōs; from an obsol. phaō (to *shine* or make *manifest*, espec. by *rays*."[3.25]

So here again the *lampo* is the cause, and the *phōs* is the result; here with *lampo* applying *first* to the face of Jesus; and *then* causing *phōs* to His clothing—respectively.

But there is a "fly in the ointment" here. The translation states: "*his raiment was white as the light*." This is presented as a *simile*, with the comparison of His "*raiment*;" with the "*light*" or *phōs*. But since it was His "raiment" itself that became *phōs*; there is no other *phōs* in these passages with which to compare, only *lampō*. To state that *phōs* was as white as the very same *phōs*, seems to provide little revelation. Thus there seems to be a *translational* error in the presentation of this as a *simile*.

The actual Greek word translated as "*as the*" is:

> "5613 hōs; prob. adv. of comp. from *3739*; *which how*, i.e. *in that manner* (very variously used, as follows)..."[3.26]

Thus: "*and His raiment was white*, (in that manner, (*hōs*)) *light*, (phōs);" seems to be a more accurate translation.

Matthew 6:22-23 (KJV) tells us:

"The light of the body is the eye:
if therefore thine eye be single,
thy whole body shall be full of light.

But if thine eye be evil, thy whole body
shall be full of darkness.
If therefore the light that is in thee be
darkness, how great is that darkness!"[3.27]

These passages begin with a preparatory *statement*: "*The light of the body is the eye.*"

There are three appearances of the translation "*light*" in these passages. Two are in verse 22, and one is in verse 23.

The original Greek word for the *first* "light," ("of the body"), in verse 22 is:

> "5460 phōtĕinŏs; from *5457*; *lustrous*, i.e. *transparent* or *well illuminated* (fig.): - bright, full of light..."[3.28]

Jesus then sets up three "if - then" scenarios.

The first is: "*if therefore thine eye be single,* (then) *thy whole body shall be full of light.*"

It must be asked precisely what is meant by one's eye being "*single*?"

The original Greek word translated as "single" is:

> "573 haplŏus; prob. from *1* (as a particle of union) and the base of *4120*; prop. *folded together*, i.e. *single* (fig. clear): - single."[3.29]

"4120 plĕkō; a prim. word; to *twine* or *braid*: - plait."[3.30]

"1 a; of Heb. or.; the first letter of the alphabet; fig. only (from its us as a numeral) the *first*: - alpha. Often used (usually an, before a vowel) also in composition as a contraction from 427) in the sense of *privation*; so in many words beginning with this letter; occasionally in the sense of *union* (as a contraction of 260)."[3.31]

It seems a bit difficult to reconcile *haplŏus* with the purported roots of "*a*" and "*plĕkō*;" which would be: "*aplĕkō*," rather than *haplŏus*. Nevertheless, the definition of *haplŏus*, indicates "single," because of: "prop. *folded together*." Thus there must initially be more than one of that which are "*folded together*," resulting in the "single."

In biology, *haploid* refers to a cell with half the number of; or single, or *unpaired* chromosomes; while *diploid* refers to the full number of; or *paired* chromosomes.

This presents an issue in that the "normal" condition of human cells, is *not* haploid, or single; but diploid or paired; yet here *haplŏus*; from which haploid is believed to be derived, means: "prop. *folded together*, i.e. *single*." Thus the use of haploid, or single, in biology refers to an *unusual* condition; while the use of whatever Aramaic word it was that was utilized by Jesus that was translated as *haplŏus*; appears to be that which should be the *normal* condition.

Nevertheless, each of these situations is preparatory for "something to happen." In the case of biology, it is human reproduction. In the case of that which it was that was spoken of by Jesus, it is: "*thy whole body shall be full of light.*"

Given the context, it would be reasonable to assume that the will of man and the will of God could be the candidates for that which are "*folded together*," resulting in the "single."

Assuming this "if" condition is met, we are told that *then*: "*thy whole body shall be full of light.*"

The original Greek word for the second "light" here in verse 22 is:

> "3088 luchnŏs; from the base of 3022; a portable *lamp* or other *illuminator* (lit. or fig.): - candle, light."[3.32]

It is not just that: "*thy whole body shall be full of light;*" as this could be *phōs*, as was the case with Jesus' raiment. Instead; this particular "light" is *luchnŏs*, which is: "a portable *lamp* or other *illuminator;*" with the key word here being "portable:" This light is moveable, and provides *illumination* wherever one may go.

In the second "if – then," we are told what will happen if it is not the case that our eye "*be*" *haplŏus*, or "*single*," because of: "prop. *folded together;*" but instead if our eye "*be evil:*" "*But if thine eye be evil, thy whole body shall be full of darkness.*"

The actual Greek word translated here as "evil" is:

> "4190 pŏnērŏs; from a der. of *4192*; *hurtful,* i.e. *evil* prop. in effect or influence..."[3.33]

In the previous chapter, evil and wicked were distinguished. Here with *pŏnērŏs,* it is unclear; as both *"evil"* and *"hurtful"* are included in the definition. However it must be noted that although *evil,* as in the sense of against God's will, may not necessarily be *wicked* to another human being; it is *"hurtful"* to God.

And the darkness in this passage as the "then," in: *"thy whole body shall be full of darkness;"* is a "relative" of the previously referenced 4655 *skŏtŏs,* and is:

> "4652 skŏtĕinŏs; from *4655 opaque,* i.e. (fig.) *benighted*: - dark, full of darkness."[3.34]

By the comparison of the "evil" eye, or *pŏnērŏs* ; with the "single" eye, *haplŏus,* or *"single,"* here because of: "prop. *folded together;*" it is obvious that this *"evil"* eye is neither "single," nor *"folded together."* Thus *double,* at a minimum; in that the two that could be "folded together" are not, but remain separate entities.

Since the one who has this "evil" or *pŏnērŏs* eye, is potentially one of the components of that which could be *haplŏus* or *"folded together;"* this seems to reasonably confirm that it is God's will, that is the other component under discussion here. You are either *with* him, *haplŏus*; or not with him because one is *pŏnērŏs*, "evil" or "hurtful."

And with *haplŏus,* the result is: "*thy whole body shall be full of light;*" and this light or *luchnŏs*, and by definition this "*luchnŏs* light" is "portable." But with *pŏnērŏs*, the result is: "*thy whole body shall be full of darkness;*" and this "*darkness*" is not from the absence of available light, but rather from "opacity."

Jesus then offers the *third* "if - then;" which is contingent upon the *second*, (eye be "*evil*"), having been met; with this "then," presented as a question: "*If therefore the light that is in thee be darkness, how great is that darkness!*" [Exclamation point noted!]

The original Greek word for the appearance of "light," here in verse 23 is again: "5457 phōs; from an obsol. phaō (to *shine* or make *manifest*, espec. by *rays*..."[3.35]

And the two mentions of "darkness" in this verse are both:

> "4655 skŏtŏs; from the base of *4639*; *shadiness*, i.e. *obscurity* (lit. or fig.): -darkness."[3.36]

One might fairly ask how it is that *light* could be *darkness*—which is a required stipulation in the very asking of this part of the question, if: "*the light that is in thee be darkness.*" But this is not what is actually stated, except by the translators.

What is actually stated as this "stipulation," is that *phōs*, or: "(to *shine* or make *manifest*, espec. by *rays*;" can be shaded or obscured, *skŏtŏs*, or: "*shadiness*, i.e. *obscurity*."

Thus the question would be better stated in English as: "If therefore the light that is in thee be *shaded* or *obscured*; how great is that *shading* or *obscuring!*"

The very next verse that follows; seems to provide the answer to this question.

Matthew 6:24 (KJV) tells us:

> "*No man can serve two masters:*
> *for either he will hate the one,*
> *and love the other;*
> *or else he will hold to the one,*
> *and despise the other.*
> *Ye cannot serve*
> *God and mammon.*"[3.37]

The Greek word translated as "mammon" is:

> "3126 mammōnas; of Chald. or. (*confidence*, i.e. fig. *wealth*, personified); *mammonas*, i.e. *avarice* (deified): - mammon."[3.38]

Avarice is another word not often seen today; and roughly means greed for material wealth. Here the reference is not to mere greed, but to the *deification* of this *avarice*. It does not appear that the Greek root of *mammon*, is synonymous with wealth alone, despite this common belief and frequent usage of mammon. It is unclear why "*confidence*" appears in this definition. Perhaps this "*confidence*" is because of this personification of "*wealth*;" and the deification of "*avarice*."

It is also unclear, as to why the *translators* did not translate *mammōnas* as *avarice*, or another relatively synonymous English word.

Although the context of these passages is in general regarding the *acquisition* of material wealth, the answer to this question is always the same. One cannot serve both upright and evil at the same time, and for the reasons given. One can only *think* they can. And it must be remembered that it is never the *money*, but the *love* of money that causes all of the problems.

Gladness was previously defined as "bright, shining;" and *gay* is similarly defined. Again, what is the difference? With *gladness*, the "bright, shining" is cause by and thus is a *reflection* of that which is *within*, and as stated, is thus limited to that which is within.

But with regard to *gay*, the bright, and shining the is result of that which is *without*; and thus is not limited by that which is within—except for cooperation with that which is without. And if one's eye is "*single*," or *haplŏus*: "prop. *folded together*;" here meaning the *will* of any H. Sapiens, and the *will* of God; the result is: "*thy whole body shall be full of light*;" and this light is *luchnŏs*; and by definition this "*luchnŏs* light" is "portable."

As previously discussed, in the KJV the word "gay" as a *translation*, appears only once.

This one appearance again is: "2985 lampas; from *2989*; a "*lamp*" or *flambeau*: - lamp, light, torch." And *lampas* is derived from: "2989 lampō a prim. verb; to *beam*, i.e. *radiate* brilliancy (lit. or fig): - give light, shine."

And if one adds in the *portability*, we have: "3088 luchnŏs; from the base of *3022*; a portable *lamp* or other *illuminator* (lit. or fig.): - candle, light."

In the literal understanding of the true *gay*, it is clear that it is God's will that all are gay; arguably by the very definition.

Gay is fun, and you get a lot more done.

4

The Purpose of Man

It would be so easy to say that the answer to the question: "What is the purpose of man?" depends upon precisely whom it is that is asked. But of course, this cannot be so. There can be only one true answer as to the purpose of man; and that is that *actual* purpose or purposes for which God Himself *created* man.

Different religions proffer various ideas regarding this. Some claim that the purpose of the earth is a place for man to live for eternity in bliss. Perhaps this is so, but it must be asked from precisely where this idea was derived.

Secular sources have various different viewpoints ranging from: "dying with the most toys," to theories that make even less sense.

The "man" occupied world has spent much of its time in substantial misery—at least with regard to the condition of man. And this condition of man often provides the fodder for many to question the existence of God; and/or His nature. After all, with the various messes the earth has been in for so much of the time, who needs a God? "I can mess things up my self—thank you very much. I don't need any help."

So precisely when and how did all of this start? If it can be stipulated that the Bible may have something of value to say about this matter; then perhaps some knowledge and subsequent wisdom can be attained.

The Bible tells us it all started: "In the beginning."

Genesis 1:1 (KJV) tells us:

> "*In the beginning God created the heaven and the earth.*"[4.1]

Precisely what is this "in the beginning?"

The actual original Hebrew word translated as: "*in the beginning*" is:

> "7225 rê'shîyth; from the same as 7218; the first, in place, time, order or rank (spec. a firstfruit)...."[4.2]

In order to have any type of *sequencing*, such as "the first," there must be *time*. Science tells us of the "Big Bang;" before which there was no time, no space, and no matter. Thus when this event occurred, (Big Bang); this represented the bringing into existence of the three, (time, space, and matter); or the bringing into existence of the *material* realm.

Thus if it is stipulated that the word "*heaven*" here in Genesis 1:1 cannot be the same "heaven" God "art in;" by Hobson's choice, this "*heaven*" must refer to the space in the *material* realm. In addition, God could not have resided in a yet to be created realm before He created the same.

So there was initially by definition an *immaterial* realm, with no time, space, or matter; and necessarily from that realm, God created a (*material*) realm, with time, space, and matter. Thus Genesis 1:1, and the "Big Bang;" represent the very same event.

What type of matter did God utilize in creating the material realm? The answer is none, because no matter existed prior to the creation of matter. Thus God did not *form*, *fashion*, or *mold* the material realm from matter, He *created* it.

The actual Hebrew word translated here as "created" is:

> "1254 bârâ', a prim. root; (absol.) to create; (qualified) to cut down (a wood), select, feed (as formative processes): - choose, create (creator), cut down, dispatch, do, make (fat)."[4.3]

> "The verb expresses creation out of nothing..."[4.4]

And we are told that the creation of the earth was completed at the end of Genesis 1:1.

But the beginning of the very next verse and onward, tells us of an entirely different situation.

Genesis 1:2 (KJV) tells us:

> "*And the earth was without form, and void; and darkness was upon the face of the deep. And the Spirit of God moved upon the face of the waters.*"[4.5]

The Interlinear Bible states: "she became;"[4.6] thus indicating a change from the conclusion of Genesis 1:1. Thus in continuous form this would read: "*In the beginning God created the heaven and the earth,*" and "*she became,*" (after earth's creation was completed), *without form* and *void.*"

In order to better understand what took place here; and most particularly man's future role in the same; it would be prudent to bypass what God Himself began doing at that time, and "jump ahead" to the entrance of man on to the scene. [For a full analysis of God's actions *before* creating man see: "*MeekRaker Beginnings...*"]

Genesis 1:26 (KJV) tells us:

"And God said, Let us make man
in our image, after our likeness:
and let them have dominion
over the fish of the sea,
and over the fowl of the air,
and over the cattle, and over all the
earth, and over every creeping thing
that creepeth upon the earth."[4.7]

Here in Genesis 1:26, God "announces" His intentions, and the very next verse, tells us what God in fact did.

Genesis 1:27 (KJV) tells us:

"So God created man in his own image,
in the image of God created he him;
male and female created he them."[4.8]

After first *announcing* His intentions, including His intention to grant man "*dominion*;" God then *created* man: "*in his own image*," and in the "*image of God*." Here we are *twice* told precisely whom it was that man "took after"—lest anyone in the future claiming to represent God or otherwise, suggest differently.

The actual original Hebrew word translated as "have dominion" in verse 26 is:

> "7287 râdâh; a prim. root; to *tread* down, i.e. *subjugate*; spec. to *crumble*

> off: - (come to, make to) have dominion, prevail against..."[4.9]

And we are then *three* times told in verse 27, precisely *how* it was that God brought man into existence: "*God created man,*" "*God created he him,*" and "*male and female created he them.*" It seems that God wanted to be sure all knew precisely *how* these "created creatures" were brought into existence—lest anyone in the future claiming to represent God or otherwise, *confuse* this with another event, which they did, (would *later* do).

So what is or are, the word or words, translated as "*created*" three times in this verse."

The actual Hebrew word appearing three times, and *translated* three times as "*created;*" is the aforementioned *bârâ'*.[4.10]

When God *created* the *material* realm, with time, space, and matter; this was *bârâ'*. There was nothing *material* utilized, as there was nothing *material* yet in existence *to* utilize.

Here when God *created* man, it is likewise *bârâ'*. But unlike when He *created* the *material* realm, here; although God *could* have utilized *matter* in causing man to come into existence, as matter *did* exist at this time; He did not—at least not for the events described in *these* passages.

In the very next verse, God then "charges," created man; telling them *collectively*, precisely what it is He wants them to do. Thus that which is contained therein, represents God's primary will with regard to man.

Genesis 1:28 (KJV) tells us:

"And God blessed them,
and God said unto them,
Be fruitful, and multiply,
and replenish the earth, and subdue it:
and have dominion over the fish of
the sea, and over the fowl of the air,
and over every living thing
that moveth upon the earth."[4.11]

This seems a rather peculiar thing for God to do, given that He is *omniscient*, *omnipotent*, and *omnipresent*. If as many believe, the earth was not actually completed at the end of Genesis 1:1, despite what we are literally told; "subdue" seems a strange request or order by God, for man's assistance in the completion of the same.

As previously addressed, some believe that God sends us "challenges" to make us "better;" and likely some would try to proffer Genesis 1:28 in furtherance of this theory. But there is that pesky: "*in his own image*," and in the "*image of God*," part.

It is also unclear how a perfect being could be capable of creating any imperfection. Stated differently, precisely how could any *subset* of the *set* "perfect," contain that which is imperfect.

And finally, if this "challenges in order to improve" theory had any factual basis, then it seems there would be some commonality between some actions of God, and some actions of Satan.

This "*subdue*" part, is especially problematic, given the actual Hebrew word *translated* here as "*subdue*."

This actual Hebrew word translated here as "subdue" is:

> "3533 kâbash; a prim. root; to *tread* down; hence neg. to *disregard*; pos. to *conquer, subjugate, violate*: - bring into bondage, force, keep under, subdue, bring into subjection."[4.12]

The "*it*" in "*and subdue it*," contextually clearly refers to the *earth*. Thus God's will with regard to man is to: "to *tread* down" and "*conquer, subjugate, violate*" the earth. The English word *kibosh*, as in: "put the kibosh on it," is derived from the Hebrew *kâbash*.

So it must be asked as to why God would create a world that was so imperfect, that He later had to create man in order to finish the job for him? The answer is that He did not do so; and likely could not have done so.

Before examining precisely what happened between Genesis 1:1 and Genesis 1:2, that caused the earth to require *kâbash*; it should be asked if there is any other evidence to support that that which is contained in the above Genesis 1:28, is in fact how it reasonably reads.

Genesis 2:1 tells us:

"Thus the heavens and the earth
were finished,
and all the host of them."[4.13]

There are two statements that are made here: "*Thus the heavens and the earth were finished,*" and: "*and all the host of them.*" These should each be addressed separately.

With regard to: "*the heavens and the earth were finished,*" the actual Hebrew word translated as "finished" is:

> "3615 kâlâh; a prim. root; to *end*, whether intrans. (to *cease, be finished, perish*) or trans. (to *complete, prepare, consume*)..."[4.14]

It would be easy to simply say: "See, the earth wasn't finished until Genesis 2:1." But "*finished*" or *kâlâh*, can refer to *any* type of *process* or *processes*. Here in Genesis 2:1, it is *both* the "*heavens and the earth;*" "*and,*" (not "or"); "*the host of them*" that we are told were "*finished,*" or *kâlâh*. Thus this statement could not have been true, until that which took place in Genesis 1:27, (the creation of man), had also been "*finished.*"

No one argues that God "did a bunch of stuff," after Genesis 1:1; and the passages that immediately follow Genesis 2:1, provide some insight into this in the very *general* sense.

The verses immediately following Genesis 1:1, here Genesis 2:2-4, (KJV) tell us:

"And on the seventh day
God ended his work which he had made;
and he rested on the seventh day

from all his work which he had made.

And God blessed the seventh day,
and sanctified it: because that in it he
had rested from all his work which
God created and made.

These are the generations of the heavens
and of the earth when they were created,
in the day that the Lord God made
the earth and the heavens,"[4.15]

In Genesis 2:2, the word "*made*" appears twice.

In Genesis 2:3, the words "*created*" and "*made*" each appear once.

In Genesis 2:4, the words "*created*" and "*made*" each appear once.

It must be asked why these two different words appear? Culinary novices often will state they *made* something; but when the result is dubious, it is often then referred to as their *creation*.

The original Hebrew word translated as "made" each time is:

> "6213 ʿâsâh; a prim. root; to do or make, in the broadest sense and widest application..."[4.16]

The original Hebrew word translated as "created" each time is the aforementioned 1254 *bârâʾ*.[4.17]

In the case of *'âsâh*, this could refer to anything "*made*: "in the broadest sense and widest application..." Thus *bârâ'* could technically fit into the definition of *'âsâh*.

But although *bârâ'* could technically fit into the definition of *'âsâh*; not all *'âsâh* is *bârâ'*.

Meaning that: "to do or make, in the broadest sense and widest application...;" includes *all* means of "making," whether *matter* was utilized or was not. But *bârâ'* requires that *nothing* material be utilized—as in the creation of the universe, where as previously stated, there was no matter available at that "time" to be used.

Thus with regard to these passages, it seems that distinctions are being made with respect to whether or not matter could have been utilized in the process. When the translation as "*created*," (bârâ'), appears; this *precludes* the use of matter. When the translation as "*made*," ('âsâh), appears; this generally includes the use of matter, but also does not necessarily preclude *bârâ'*.

Therefore, it seems reasonable that since *both* of these words appear in these passages; "*made*," as *'âsâh*; likely refers to the use of matter in the process; and "*created*," as *bârâ'*; likely refers to a process where matter was not utilized.

So it must be asked precisely what it is we are told was "finished" when we are told in Genesis 2:1: "*Thus the heavens and the earth were finished*," and: "*and all the host of them*."

There are *three* distinct things under discussion in these verses. The first is the *creation*, or *bârâ'* of the heavens and the earth. The second in whatever

God "*made,*" or *'âsâh* . And the third is the *creation*, or *bârâ'* of man. Thus it seems what was "*finished,*" includes all three; and not just the *creation*, or *bârâ'* of the heavens and the earth.

And as will be seen, the "*finished*" is from God's perspective and role only; and not from the perspective of the final product; i.e.; the condition of the earth at that time.

In verse 2 we are told "*And on the seventh day God ended his work which he had made; and he rested on the seventh day from all his work which he had made.*" This passage literally refers to only what God "made;" and not what He "created"—something which is then confirmed in verse 3.

Verse 3 tells us: "*And God blessed the seventh day, and sanctified it: because that in it he had rested from all his work which God created and made.*" Here the distinction is made, by the inclusion of both "*created*" and "*made.*"

But does this make any degree sense? We are told here that God "*blessed*" and "*sanctified*" the "*seventh day;*" "*because*" He "*rested.*"

A word about the translation as: "*day.*" Most believe that the use of "*day*" here; represents a *literal* twenty four hour day. However, the word "day" can also relate to a period of *activity*, (*chiros*); as well as a fixed period of *time*, (*kronos* or *chronos*).

The actual Hebrew word translated as "day" is:

> "3117 yôwm; from an unused root mean. to *be hot*; a *day* (as the *warm* hours), whether lit. (from sunrise to

> sunset, or from one sunset to the next), or fig. (a space of time defined by an associated term), [often used adv.]..."[4.18]

Thus it could be the case that this "rested," likely signified the end of the period of *activity*, rather than the twenty four hour "*day*." And what was that activity? That period of activity was all: "*God created and made*," up to that period of time.

The "*created*," (*bârâ'*), part; includes the creation of the heavens and the earth, man; as well as some other action that will be addressed shortly.

The "*made*," ('âsâh), part; refers to actions God undertook other than literal creation.

And finally, verse 4 tells us: "*These are the generations of the heavens and of the earth when they were created, in the day that the Lord God made the earth and the heavens*."

Here "*created*" is: "bârâ';"[4.19] and "*made*" is: "'âsâh."[4.20]

The actual Hebrew word translated as "generations" is:

> "8435 tôwl^{e}dâh; or tôl^{e}dâh; from 3205; (plur. only) *descent*, i.e. *family*; (fig.) *history*: - birth, generations."[4.21]

Contextually, it seems that the *figurative* meaning of *tôwl^{e}dâh* as *history*, is what is meant here. Thus these are the history(ies) "*of the heavens and of the earth when they were created*," seems to be the most reasonable meaning. And when was this history *provided*? This is or was provided: "*in the day that the Lord God made the earth and the heavens.*" Here the "*made*" refers to actions other than creation.

To the likely surprise of many, God did not actually do all that much actual creating in Genesis 1. In fact the word *bârâ'* appears only five times in Genesis 1. The creation of the heavens and the earth is the *first* appearance. The creation of man is the *second*, *third*, and *fourth* appearance.

And the final appearance of *bârâ'* is in Genesis 1:21 (KJV):

"*And God created great whales,*
and every living creature that moveth,
which the waters brought forth abundantly,
after their kind, and every
winged fowl after his kind:
and God saw that it was good."[4.22]

Thus up until the beginning of these Genesis 2 passages, all other actions taken by God could reasonably be placed in the "made;" or "6213 ʻâsâh; a prim. root; to do or make, in the broadest sense and widest application..." category.

And what about the *second* half of Genesis 2:1: "*and all the host of them.*" In context, again this is: "*Thus the heavens and the earth were finished, and all the host of them.*"

The actual word translated as "host" is:

> "6635 tsâbâ' or ts^{e}bâ'âh from 6633; a *mass* of persons (or fig. things), espec. reg. organized for war (an *army*); by impl. a *campaign*, lit. or fig. (spec. *hardship, worship*): -appointed time, (+) army, (+) battle, company, host, service, soldiers, waiting upon, war (fare)."[4.23]

It is God *Himself* who is referring to created man as: "a *mass* of persons (or fig. things), espec. reg. organized for war (an *army*)."

This term *tsâbâ'* is perfectly consistent with God's expressed *desire* as stated in Genesis 1:26, to give man "*dominion*," or *râdâh*, "*over the earth*;" and the instructions God gave man in Genesis 1:28: to "*subdue*" or: "kâbash; a prim. root; to *tread* down; hence neg. to *disregard*; pos. to *conquer, subjugate, violate*: - bring into bondage, force, keep under, subdue, bring into subjection;" the earth.

Tsâbâ' is seen elsewhere in the Bible.

Numbers 2:3-4 (KJV) tell us:

"And on the east side toward the rising
of the sun shall they of the standard
of the camp of Judah pitch throughout
their armies: and Nahshon
the son of Amminadab
shall be captain of the children of Judah.

And his host, and those that
were numbered of them,

were threescore and fourteen
thousand and six hundred."[4.24]

Here in Numbers, the word translated as "*armies*" and "*host*," is *tsâbâ'*. Originally, the translation of *tsâbâ'* in verse 3 was also "host."[4.25]

2 Samuel 10:6-7 (KJV) tells us:

"*And when the children of Ammon*
saw that they stank before David,
the children of Ammon sent and hired the
Syrians of Bethrehob and the Syrians of Zoba,
twenty thousand footmen,
and of king Maacah a thousand men,
and of Ishtob twelve thousand men.

And when David heard of it, he sent Joab,
and all the host of the mighty men."[4.26]

Here in 2 Samuel, the word translated as "*host*," is *tsâbâ'*.[4.27]

As can easily be seen, the: "*the heavens and the earth were finished*," in no way refers to the *condition* of the earth—else why did God create *tsâbâ'*, and then instruct these *tsâbâ'* to *kâbash* the earth? God's role *in this particular matter* was finished, but it was the job of *tsâbâ'* to continue the process.

What was it that happened, that required God to create man for the purpose of *tsâbâ*? This actually represents two questions:

The first question, is what happened that necessitated that man be *created* with the stated purpose to: "*have dominion*," or *râdâh*; literally: "to *tread* down, i.e. *subjugate*; spec. to *crumble* off: - (come to, make to) have dominion, prevail against...," "*over all the earth*;" and then *after* being *created*, be then instructed by God to "*subdue*," or *kâbash*; literally: "to *tread* down; hence neg. to *disregard*; pos. to *conquer*, *subjugate*, *violate*: - bring into bondage, force, keep under, subdue, bring into subjection;" the earth?

And the second question is why God did not simply do this all Himself?

5

The Source of the Problem

Following is an excerpt from Danté Camminatore's: "*Causando un Posto per Loro [Causing a Place for Them]*," contained in: "*Ostium Ab Inferno—The Opening From Hell.*" [Reprinted by Permission.]

"Revelation 12:7-9 (KJV) tells us:

"And there was war
in heaven:
Michael and his Angels
fought against the

dragon; and the dragon
fought and his angels,

And prevailed not; neither
was their place found
any more in heaven.

And the great dragon
was cast out,
that old serpent, called
the Devil, and Satan,
which deceiveth the
whole world: he was cast
out into the earth,
and his angels were
cast out with him."[OAI3]

"Here we have a description of what happened; (most likely at some point in time between Genesis 1:1 and Genesis 1:2); when sin attempted to contaminate the *immaterial* realm or heaven. Although very little is known regarding the circumstances surrounding this battle, what is clear is that there was then no place "any more" for the enemy or "his angels" in the immaterial realm or "heaven," and they were "cast out."

"The actual Greek word translated as "angels" is:

> "32 aggĕlŏs; from aggĕllō; (prob. der. from 71; comp. 34) (to *bring tidings*); a *messenger*; esp. an "*angel*"; by impl. a *pastor*:- angel, messenger."[OAI4]

"The word *aggĕlŏs* is the only word used for "angels" in the entire New Testament, except in Luke 20:36 which is:

> "2465 isaggĕlŏs; from 2470 and 32; *like an angel*, i.e. *angelic*: - equal unto the angels."[OAI5]

"Just for reference, Luke 20:36 (KJV) tells us:

> "*Neither can they die any more: for they are equal unto the angels; and are the children of God, being the children of the resurrection.*"[OAI6]

"The definition of the aggĕlŏs requires three things. First; one who sends a message or tidings. Second; the message or tidings itself or themselves. And third; a recipient for the message or tidings. The significance of this will be addressed later.

"It must be noted that the actual Greek word translated as "deceiveth" is:

> "4105 planaō; from *4106*; to (prop. *cause to*) *roam* (from safety, truth, or virtue): - go astray, deceive, err, seduce, wander, be out of the way."[OAI7]

"Thus here there are actually two matters to consider. The *objective of* these particular aggĕlŏs, is or was planaō; or "to (prop. *cause to*) *roam* (from safety, truth, or virtue): - go astray, deceive, err, seduce, wander, be out of the way." The "these," in this context, is important because not all angels or aggĕlŏs seek planaō. It was only *these particular* angels or aggĕlŏs; those "cast out with him;" who sought and seek planaō. Those who were not "cast out;" i.e.; are not with the enemy, are likewise aggĕlŏs; but they do not seek planaō.

"As an aside, it is considered "common knowledge" or *doxa* that the enemy took *one third* of the angels with him; however there seems to be little Biblical evidence for this.

"Revelation 12:4 is usually cited as the source for this "took one third" belief:

"Revelation 12:4 (KJV) tells us:

"And his tail drew the
third part of the stars of
heaven, and did cast
them to the earth:
and the dragon stood
before the woman which
was ready to be
delivered, for to devour
her child as soon as it
was born."[OAI8]

"There are several problems with citing this verse as evidence for the "one third" theory. Revelation 12:9 tells us the enemy: "*was cast out into the earth, and his angels were cast out with him.*" Thus it was not the enemy who did any casting out of these *aggĕlŏs*; whether by utilizing his tail, or by any other means—they were "thrown out" together.

"Neither Satan nor these aggĕlŏs were active parties in this expulsion event; i.e.; they were the "baseballs" and not the "batter." And given the context, the timing is way off, unless one believes that "*the woman which was ready to be delivered, for to devour her child as soon as it was born*;" had already occurred long long ago. And also given the context, it seems that this "tail action" relates to an entirely different event, and an event in the far future.

"There are both similarities and differences with respect to the enemy and a contaminated soul:

"The enemy was *cast out* of the immaterial realm; (*heaven* but not the heavens); because of the contamination of sin committed while in that realm. The actual word here in this passage of Revelation translated as "into" is:

> "*1519* ĕis *to* or *into* (indicating the point reached or entered) of place, time, or (fig) purpose (result etc.)"[OAI9]

"So at this point it is unclear whether "to the earth" or "into the earth" represents the correct translation.

"Man is refused *reentry*, because of sin committed while in the condition of physical life.

"Although the actual genesis of the enemy is not known, it seems clear that the enemy is an immaterial entity, and was designed to exist, and did in fact exist, in the immaterial realm; and thus was not designed to exist in the material realm. We are told that he was cast out of the immaterial realm, either *to* the earth or *into* the earth. But as a *material* entity on the *material* realm, the enemy is not generally recognizable as such.

"At the risk of a "double tautology," it must again be stated that the immaterial part of man is immaterial in nature, and the material part of man is material. The true part or essence of man (the part that is created equal), is the immaterial part; with the material part representing a vessel for earthly (material) existence. The immaterial part is immortal, but the physical part, under normal circumstances, is not—at least by the "normal" rules of the material realm.

"For clarity, distinctions must be made. It is beyond any rational dispute, that there is an immaterial realm with "current lawful occupants." God and angels (*non-planaō* seeking angels) come to mind first. To the extent that there are other *immaterial* entities that exist, these either "lawfully reside" in the immaterial realm as per design, or they do not. To be clear, this: "do not" does not mean *unlawful* residence in the immaterial realm, as we are told what happens when this is attempted. This refers to immaterial entities that may in fact exist, but do not exist or "reside" in the immaterial realm. There may be a plethora of other entities legitimately residing in the immaterial realm, or there may not be. However the enemy and "his angels" although they continue to exist, we are told they no longer reside in the immaterial realm as they by design should—and by design they do not possess an earthly vessel, and thus cannot have any type of "normal material" existence.

"The material and immaterial realms are a binary; in that there is either matter or there is not. Any entity who either cannot re-enter the immaterial realm (contaminated soul); or one who was "cast out" of the immaterial realm, cannot exist in or on that realm. And if *neither* has the physical vessel to exist in the material realm; e.g.; an entity originally designed for immaterial existence, or a soul departed from said physical vessel (no longer has an "earth suit"); then neither can either of the same truly exist in the material realm.

"The "nether world" is generally considered to be that which is down or beneath the surface of the earth; arguably the "bad section" of the *immaterial* realm; with perhaps the surface of the earth being the "tracks" which this nether world is on the "bad side" of. This would be consistent with the "cast out *into* the earth" translation of the aforementioned *ĕis*.

"Merriam Webster defines "nether" as:

> "1: situated down or below: lower; 2: situated or believed to be situated beneath the earth's surface."[OAI10]

"But although this "nether world" may not be material, "neither" is it necessarily any part of the immaterial realm.

"It could in fact be; any "etymological sources" to the contrary not withstanding; that this "nether" merely represents a misspelling of "neither."

"If so, this would represent both a kind of third realm; and *not* a third realm simultaneously. Meaning; that the "*neither world;*" as opposed to the common usage of "*nether* world;" actually means *neither* realm or "world;" or "stuck" between the two realms. This would be an "X realm;" and is not *either* realm; but rather *neither* realm, or *no realm*.

"This may have been the actual source of the now abandoned concept of "Limbo." The Catholic doctrine of Limbo was concerned with that place where those who were not "Baptized;" usually infants; supposedly went upon physical death. The belief is or was; that *all* (except Jesus) are born with "original sin," which is removed only with Baptism. Since the belief is that no one can go to heaven unless cleansed of this and all other sins; there then had to be a place for infants who are all born with original sin; but yet could not have sinned of their own free will. No attempt is being made here to attest to the truth or falsity of any particular religious beliefs, including this one; but merely to present them.

"Thus this concept of "Limbo" represented a destination between heaven and hell. According to this doctrine, the infant *could* not go to heaven because of the original sin; yet *should* not go to hell because infants do not know right from wrong, and thus cannot sin of their own free will. Hence there had to be a benign place that was in the immaterial realm, but technically not part of "heaven."

"However; it is possible that originally this concept of "Limbo" referred to not a section of the *immaterial* realm outside of heaven, but rather to be caught *in between* the material and immaterial realms—this *neither* world, AKA: the "X" or the "no realm."

"The word "limbo" can refer to either a dance which was popular in the 1950's and/or the 1960's; or it refers to something else. That something else can be seen from the root of the word.

"Limbo is derived from:

> "Latin (in) *limbō* (on) the edge, ablative case of *limbus* edge, border..."[OAI11]

"Limbo originally likely meant this border or edge between the two realms; rather than a separate place within a realm; here a separate "place" as or like the immaterial realm; in terms of including no space, time, or matter; but not actually within either realm. This can also be seen with the common usage of "stuck in limbo;" which means stuck between two things, and unable to move forward or backward.

"The common concept (doxa) of "hell" requires a bit of analysis. It is generally considered as a possible destination for the immaterial portion of life forms—those with the "breath of life." However the origin of the word "hell" seems a bit sketchy.

"According to Etymonline.com, "hell" is from:

> "Old English hel, helle, "nether world, abode of the dead, infernal regions, place of torment for the wicked after death," from Proto-Germanic *haljō "the underworld" (source also of Old Frisian helle, Old Saxon hellia, Dutch hel, Old Norse hel, German Hölle, Gothic halja "hell").
>
> "Literally"concealed place" (compare Old Norse hellir "cave, cavern"), from PIE

> root *kel-(1) "to cover, conceal, save." The English word may be in part from Old Norse mythological Hel (from Proto-Germanic *halija "one who covers up or hides something"), in Norse mythology the name of Loki's daughter who rules over the evil dead in Niflheim, the lowest of all worlds (nifl "mist"). A pagan concept and word fitted to a Christian idiom.
>
> "In Middle English, also of the Limbus Patrum, place where the Patriarchs, Prophets, etc. awaited the Atonement."[OAI12]

"It should be noted here that the etymology of "atone," is actually the fusion of the words "at" and "one." Here we have the use of Limbus Patrum, or the limbo of the fathers in the description and etymology of hell? What is this Limbus Patrum? This is the "place" where the immaterial part of those "Patriarchs, Prophets, etc.;" i.e.; those great men of the Bible;

"went" because salvation was unavailable to them while they were physically alive. Arguably this is a *temporary* condition, unlike the purported concept of limbo for un-baptized children. So if you lived *before* Jesus provided salvation; and having committed all types of sins, you were sent to a *temporary* limbo. But with this "original sin and Limbo" theory, if you were born after salvation was available, and having been incapable of sinning, but remained uncleansed of original sin; this limbo was *permanent*.

"It seems that the original meaning of hell had much more to do with a "concealed place" or "to cover, conceal;" rather than a fiery place where some souls go for eternal punishment. It must be asked as to precisely from what it is that this "place" known as hell provides concealment? It could metaphorically be asked if twilight conceals the dark from the light; or if twilight conceals the light from the dark.

"The use of the term infernal:

> "*adj*. about 1385 *infernal* of hell, in Chaucer's *Canterbury Tales*; borrowed from Old

> French *infernal*, from Late Latin *īnfernālis* belonging to the lower regions, from *īnfernus* hell, literally, the lower world, noun use of Latin *īnfernus* situated below, of the lower regions, lower, related to *īnfernus* below; see UNDER."[OAI13]

"Likely the idea of inferno representing a hot or fiery area, was the result of the conflating of the hot "lower regions," or what is "UNDER" the material earth, with this immaterial-like "place;" that is neither within the immaterial realm or heaven; nor is it a part of the material realm.

""Into the earth" in the literal *material* sense, means substantial increases in temperature; i.e.; as calculable per the *geothermal gradient*. But since heat as we know it is the movement of material phenomena, it seems difficult to conceive of heat in any realm or world without matter.

"As previously stated, there are two types of "death." There is *physical* death: where the soul et al. is no longer "contained" in the body. There is also so called *spiritual* death: where after physical death, this soul cannot be (re)connected to or in the presence of God because of sin. Cemeteries, mausoleums and the like; are generally not considered as in any way synonymous with hell. Thus, the above definition of hell as "abode of the dead" cannot in any way refer to the abode of the *material* portion of man. Ergo, it is only the *immaterial* portion of man which can abide in hell. But the immaterial portion of man is immortal; else how could there be eternal punishment in hell; or eternal happiness in heaven? It can and should be fairly asked how it could be that this immaterial portion of man could actually die? The answer is that it does not. This "death" is spiritual death, and refers to the immaterial portion not being connected to or in the presence of God after physical death.

"If it is stipulated that this nether (neither) world is as it appears to be, then whether called nether world, hell or limbo; it represents a "place" "where" immaterial entities reside that is in between the two (material and immaterial) realms. That which is in this neither or nether world; is concealed from both the material and the immaterial realms.

> "Thus at least conceptually, there must be at least two "edges" or "borders" ["Latin (in) limbō (on) the edge, ablative case of limbus edge, border..."] providing this area of "concealment." One "edge" or "border" conceals this area from the immaterial realm, and prevents entrance to the same. And the other conceals this area from the material realm, and prevents entrance into the same.
>
> "The desired result by design, is that any entity present "there," is "stuck" in between the two realms, and cannot of his own choosing move into either the material or the immaterial realm..."[5.1]

Back in Chapter 2, the word translated as "*error*" in Romans 1:27 (KJV): "*receiving in themselves that recompence of their error which was meet*;" was: "4106 planē; fem. of *4108* (as abstr.); obj. *fraudulence*; subj. a *straying* from orthodoxy or piety..."

Planē is the root of the previously cited word translated here in Revelation as "deceiveth: "4105 planaō; from *4106*; to (prop. *cause to*) *roam* (from safety, truth, or virtue): - go astray, deceive, err, seduce, wander, be out of the way."

In keeping with subject of the "spiritual death" portion of this excerpt, there is another event that should be addressed. After God, *created* man in Genesis 1:27; *charged* man with his duties in Genesis 1:28; and stated: "*Thus the heavens and the earth were finished, and all the host of them*" in Genesis 2:1; God then did something *similar* to the creation of man. The end result was essentially the same, but He did so in an entirely *different* manner.

Genesis 2:7 (KJV) tells us:

> "*And the Lord God formed man*
> *of the dust of the ground,*
> *and breathed into his nostrils*
> *the breath of life;*
> *and man became a living soul.*"[5.2]

The first thing that must be noted; is that we are told that God did not *create* this man, who would later be known as Adam, from *nothing*—as was the case in Genesis 1:27. Instead, here God *formed* this man from available *matter*.

The original Hebrew word translated here as "formed" is not *bârâ'*, as was the case for the previously *created* hosts; but rather is:

> "3335 yâtsar; prob. identical with 3334 (through the *squeezing* into shape); ([comp. 3331]); to *mould* into a form; espec. as a *potter*;..."[5.3]

In order for there to be *yâtsar*, there must be matter to "*mould* into a form;" and we are told what this matter was.

The actual Hebrew word for this *matter*, translated here as "dust" is:

> "6083 'âphâr from 6080; dust (as powdered or gray); hence clay, earth, mud: - ashes, dust, earth, ground, morter, powder, rubbish."[5.4]

And then in the very next verse, Genesis 2:8 (KJV) we are told:

> "*And the Lord God planted a garden*
> *eastward in Eden;*
> *and there he put the man*
> *whom he had formed.*"[5.5]

We are not told merely that "*the man*" was put there; but rather "*the man whom he had formed.*" This is to insure that this *formed* "man," is distinguished from the *created* man in Genesis 1:27.

It must be remembered that three of the five appearances of *bârâ'* in Genesis 1, are contained in this one, (Genesis 1:27), verse: "*So God created man in his own image, in the image of God created he him; male and female created he them.*" This is also to insure that the *created* "man" in Genesis 1:27, is easily distinguished from the *formed* man here in Genesis 2:7.

Thus the *formation* of this "man," represents an entirely different event that the *creation* of the original "*host,*" that was "*finished*" back in Genesis

2:1. However, this *formed* "*man*" did also have a role to play as *tsâbâ'*; to *kâbash* the earth. So this "man" was in fact *tsâbâ'*; but he was just not one of the original *created tsâbâ'*.

The role of this *formed* man; was to begin the bloodline for Messiah. This is why Jesus is referred to as the "last Adam."

1 Corinthians 15:45 (KJV) tells us:

> "*And so it is written, The first man Adam was made a living soul; the last Adam was made a quickening spirit.*"[5.6]

This "first Adam" *began* this redemption of *man* process; and the "last Adam" *finished* this process. It is this very *process*, that is the "it," to which Jesus referred as being "finished," at Calvary. And even if one does not believe that Messiah has already arrived, this would change nothing with respect to both the *formation* of, and the *purpose* of Adam.

God knew well in advance that no normal *tsâbâ'* was immune to effects of the *planaō* of the enemy; while engaging in subduing or *kâbash* the earth as per His instructions. Thus redemption, salvation, via justification would be necessary.

When this "man," now called Adam, exited the protected area; there were the descendants of the original created hosts present—likely the *original* Chaldeans. These "outsiders" named Adam: "one from the other side;" which is the word "Hebrew" in Chaldean. This is also likely why the Hebrew language contains so many Chaldean roots.

It is the standard assumption by many religions and "Bible scholars," that a process that *precludes* the use of matter; and a process that *requires* matter; are nevertheless somehow precisely the same event. And it is largely because of this erroneous assumption, that many proclaim quite loudly that: "according to the Bible," the earth is less than ten thousand years old.

It is true that Adam was *formed* less than ten thousand years ago; and this is reasonably known because of dates of birth of the offspring; i.e.; the "begats." And it is also true that these, (the Hebrews), were God's "chosen people." This is because as stated, they were *chosen* for the bloodline for Messiah. There is no evidence that using the term "chosen," when describing these people, has any other significance or meaning outside of this.

And it is also true, that there is no reasonable Biblical evidence as to *when* the original created hosts came into existence. Thus science would be the best source for this information. This *creative* event likely occurred hundred of thousands of years ago; and thus hundreds of millennia before the time of the *formation* of Adam.

Many believe that the book of Revelation, at least from Chapter 4 onward, is concerned only with *future* events. Thus with this view, none of that which John was permitted to "see" had yet happened at the time he "saw" it.

And so then according to this view, Satan would not have yet been "thrown down" at the time John "saw" this. This view of course presents serious problems with much other Scriptural evidence. But the truth is that in the immaterial realm there is no "time"—at least as far as the meaning of "time" is "currently" understood. What John likely "saw;" were past, present, and future; and all: "at once."

An obvious problem is developing here. If God did not create man until Genesis 1:27; but the Satan was thrown down between Genesis 1:1 and Genesis 1:2 for having already engaged in: "planaō; from *4106*; to (prop. *cause to*) *roam* (from safety, truth, or virtue): - go astray, deceive, err, seduce, wander, be out of the way;" *who* or *what* then was it that represented the *targets* or the *victims* of this *planaō*?

> "Although this is also beyond the scope of this work, the latter; (*absolute* sense; i.e.; there were in fact "material realm" deceptions occurring prior to the "casting out"); strongly suggests some type of "life form(s)" be present on the earth between Genesis 1:1 and Genesis 1:2—else what was the target of the deception? What God actually and literally did during that which is known as the "creation;" (as opposed to, and *after* conclusion of the "Beginning"); is consistent with this possibility.
>
> "Most believe that early Genesis is fraught with "creating." However an

unbiased analysis of the actual events based upon actual terminology, strongly suggests otherwise.

"Words mean things, and perfect synonyms are difficult, especially in translations. Actually, it is not certain that there are any perfect synonyms within the same language. "In the Beginning," it was the heavens and the earth that was created. In fact, the terms "created" or "creature," do not appear again in Genesis 1, until verses 21 and 20 respectively."

"This would also be consistent with the concept of beliefs regarding an Atlantis or Lemuria—at least in terms of *some* life forms being present at that time; (between Genesis 1:1 and 1:2; or between the words "*earth*" and "*without form and void*").

"Those who scoff at this idea, generally claim ignorance of plate tectonics on the part of the proponents, as the reason for this belief.

"However; although "evidence" regarding the timeframe is sketchy at best; *if* some type of continent such as Atlantis existed, it existed at a time between one million and one hundred million years ago—chronologically likely long before the *created* hosts and the kibosh (English) directive; and even longer before the *formation* of A & E. The "plates" can move substantially in one hundred million years. If something similar to Atlantis existed, it is generally believed to ultimately have become covered in water. If this sounds familiar to those who understand early Genesis, there are very good reasons for this familiarity.

"So to those who might still maintain that the *creation* of the earth was a process extending far beyond the end of Genesis 1:1, the question becomes this: Why would God create an earth that required replenishment, and subduing, (putting the kibosh on), and dominating, and then refer to created man as hosts; which is a fighting force; rather than creating an earth perfectly suitable for man? The simple answer is that He *wouldn't*; and He *didn't*.

"Most agree that the Bible is primarily a book about redemption. But few understand what this actually means; i.e.; the actual *extent* of this redemption. It is generally, (erroneously), understood; that it is solely the redemption of man with which the Bible is concerned. However; the Bible is not merely concerned with the redemption of

> man, but also the redemption of the very earth itself—perhaps even the entire material ream.
>
> "This can easily be seen in the latter half of Genesis 1:2 and onward, where God begins to take redemptive action. Then the created hosts are advised to take redemptive action. Then likely through the formation of Adam, the seeds are sown for the Son to engage in the (immaterial) redemptive process; along with, and with assistance of the hosts."[5.7]

The enemy knows all of this of course; and so he or it engages in tremendous efforts, in order to try and make certain that no host ever finds out what he or she is on the earth to do. After all, it is much easier to defeat an enemy; if said enemy has no idea there is an actual war going on. [Communist China has been utilizing this as an economic technique for decades.]

And most assuredly, the enemy does not want any host to know what weaponry is available to him. Neither does the enemy want any host to know what the enemy is afraid of.

And unfortunately, those translators of the original Hebrew and Greek have been of tremendous value to the enemy in these regards. But at least their fruit is openly known to all as "versions."

These versions often utilize *mistranslations*, *deletions*, and *additions*—whether done deliberately or otherwise.

6

Unholy Assistance

With regard to *mistranslations*; in an earlier chapter it was seen how the mistranslation of just one word; *yâda'*, changed the entire *reality* of that which happened at Sodom for billions, and for millennia—a blatant untruth, which nevertheless largely remains "common knowledge," yet today.

Without this mistranslation *euphemistically* as "sexual relations," instead of *literally* "to know;" there would not seem to be any relationship whatsoever between the events at Sodom, (or Gomorrah); and homosexuality.

It is true that it was Lot who utilized *yâda' euphemistically* when he offered females, (his own daughters), to a group that most even today believe were male homosexuals. This action would seem to make little sense, if Lot had at that time believed that these men were male homosexuals; and were utilizing *yâda'* euphemistically when speaking to him about what they wanted to do.

The result of this mistranslation of *yâda'*, was to supplant the true reasons for the destruction of Sodom with homosexuality; e.g.; "God hates homosexuality so much that He did what He did at Sodom." And as stated, the truth is that what happened at Sodom had little or nothing to do with homosexuality, except perhaps tangentially.

Although considered as sinful Biblically, homosexuality seems to be a relatively minor sin. This is known because of both the paucity of actual Biblical references; and the previously cited literal Biblical penalty for the same. And the reason for this is likely because there is no victim—if it is homosexuality alone

It is difficult to even try to ascertain the level of human misery "justified" by this one mistranslation; and the subsequent erroneous *reality* caused solely by this same one mistranslation.

Luke 8:31 (KJV) tells us:

> "*And they besought him*
> *that he would not command them*
> *to go out into the deep.*"[6.1]

This verse is part of the story of "Legion." Here the devils or "Legion," are begging Jesus to *not* do something. And given the context, this "*deep*" could lead the reader to believe that it simply refers to a part of the body of water to which they, (Legion), were ultimately sent. [Perhaps they simply lacked the ability to swim, and thus feared drowning.]

However, the original Greek word translated here as "deep" is:

> "12 abussŏs; from *1* (as a neg. particle) and a var. of *1037*; *depthless*, i.e. (spec.) (infernal) "*abyss*": - deep, (bottomless) pit."[6.2]

This same word *abussŏs*, also appears in Revelation 9:1 and 9:2 (KJV):[6.3]

> *"And the fifth angel sounded,*
> *and I saw a star fall from heaven unto*
> *the earth: and to him was given the*
> *key of the bottomless pit.*
>
> *And he opened the bottomless pit;*
> *and there arose a smoke out of the pit,*
> *as the smoke of a great furnace;*
> *and the sun and the air were darkened*
> *by reason of the smoke of the pit."*[6.4]

Here in Revelation, as can be seen; *abussŏs* is translated not as "*deep*" but as "*bottomless*."

And the actual Greek word translated here in Revelation as "pit" four times is:

> "5421 phrĕar; of uncert. der.; a *hole* in the ground (dug for obtaining or holding water or other purposes), i.e. a *cistern* or *well*; fig. an *abyss* (as a *prison*): - well, pit."[6.5]

"*Deep*" requires that a bottom exists, but that this bottom is distant. "*Bottomless*," if used *literally*; *literally* requires that no bottom exists. Yet this same word, *abussŏs*, is *translated* both ways; "deep" and "bottomless"—even though "*depthless*" is contained in the very definition of *abussŏs*.

So it must be asked why it is that in Revelation, *abussŏs* is translated as "*bottomless*," or no bottom; and yet in Luke *abussŏs* is translated as "*deep*," which requires a bottom? As will gradually become evident, the answer is *fear*.

This same story appears in Mark 5:10. But in Mark, the word *abussŏs* does not appear. Instead the *translation* is: "*he would not send them away out of the country*."[6.6]

The actual Greek word in Mark, appearing in place of *abussŏs* is:

> "5561 chōra; fem. of a der. of the base of 5490 through the idea of empty expanse; room, i.e. a space of territory (more or less extensive; often includ.

> its inhab.): - coast, county, fields, ground, land, region."[6.7]
> "5490 chasma; from a form of an obsol. prim. chaō (to "gape" or "yawn"); a "chasm" or vacancy (impassable interval): - gulf."[6.8]

There is no indication that "Legion" spoke this phrase twice to Jesus.

For Luke, the KJV translators chose "*deep*" as the translation of *abussŏs*, which actually means: "*depthless*, i.e. (spec.) (infernal) "*abyss*."

And for Mark, the KJV translators chose "*country*" as the translation of *chōra*, which actually means: "through the idea of empty expanse;" and is derived from: "chasma; from a form of an obsol. prim. chaō (to "gape" or "yawn"); a "chasm" or vacancy (impassable interval)." [It should not be overlooked that despite the translation of *chōra* as "*country*" in Mark; nevertheless "country," is not listed as a translation of *chōra*, (those words listed after the : -), anywhere in the entire Bible.]

So precisely what is it that is actually happening here?

Following are the actual pertinent passages, Luke 8:28-33 (KJV):

"When he saw Jesus, he cried out,
and fell down before him,
and with a loud voice said,
What have I to do with thee, Jesus,

thou Son of God most high?
I beseech thee, torment me not.
(For he had commanded the unclean
spirit to come out of the man.
For oftentimes it had caught him:
and he was kept bound
with chains and in fetters;
and he brake the bands, and was
driven of the devil into the wilderness.)

And Jesus asked him, saying,
What is thy name? And he said, Legion:
because many devils were entered into him.

And they besought him that he would
not command them to go out into the deep.

And there was there an herd of many
swine feeding on the mountain:
and they besought him that he
would suffer them to enter into them.
And he suffered them.

Then went the devils out of the man,
and entered into the swine:
and the herd ran violently down a steep
place into the lake, and were choked."[6.9]

The very first thing "Legion" does, is "*fell*" before Jesus; and then recognizes Jesus as the "*Son of God most high*." Legion then asks Jesus for mercy: "*torment me not*." We are then told *why* Legion is asking for mercy: "*For* (because) *he had commanded the unclean spirit to come out of the man.*" [Since these passages do not include the actual text of that which was "*commanded,*" perhaps it was non-verbal.]

By the inclusion of "*for,*" or *because*; there is a connection made between this previous command by Jesus to: "*come out of the man;*" and Legion's expectation of future "*torment.*"

After next answering Jesus' question about his name, Legion then addresses what is the likely the source of this anticipated future "*torment,*" with the same being sent to: "abussŏs; from *1* (as a neg. particle) and a var. of *1037*; *depthless*, i.e. (spec.) (infernal) "*abyss*": - deep, (bottomless) pit;" which is nevertheless translated as "*deep,*" according to KJV Luke.

Or alternatively, this "*torment,*" as the result of Legion being sent to *chōra*: "through the idea of empty expanse;" which is derived from: "chasma; from a form of an obsol. prim. chaō (to "gape" or "yawn"); a "chasm" or vacancy (impassable interval);" which is nevertheless translated as "*country,*" according to KJV Mark.

But Matthew 12:43-45 (KJV) tells us:

"*When the unclean spirit is gone out*
of a man, he walketh through dry places,
seeking rest, and findeth none.

Then he saith, I will return into my
House from whence I came out;

and when he is come, he findeth it empty, swept, and garnished.

Then goeth he, and taketh with himself seven other spirits more wicked than himself, and they enter in and dwell there: and the last state of that man is worse than the first. Even so shall it be also unto this wicked generation."[6.10]

How do these passages in Matthew comport with Legion's fear of torment in Luke? It does not seem that: "*walketh through dry places, seeking rest, and findeth none*," would in any way justify Legion's level of concern regarding future "*torment*."

The actual Greek word translated as "gone" is:

> "1831 ĕxĕrchŏmai; from *1537* and *2064*; to *issue* (lit. or fig.): - come - (forth, out), depart (out of), escape, get out..."[6.11]

Here in Matthew 12:43, we are told what happens when an "unclean spirit" *ĕxĕrchŏmai*, or *departs* a man. This has strictly to do with what happens as the result of *leaving*. This has only to do with leaving the *previous* location; and has nothing to do with any *future* location.

But Legion was concerned not with any previous location, or where he would *depart from*; but rather where he would be *sent to*.

When actions are undertaken to see to it that an: "*unclean spirit is gone out of a man*;" rarely is there any concern, other than that this "*unclean spirit*" is no longer in "*a man*." There is generally no concern for where this "*unclean spirit*" *goes*, or *is*, *afterward*; or will be in the *future*; but only that it is no longer in the "*man*." There is often much dramatic flummery about the desired future location of this "*unclean spirit*;" but this is generally insincere, as generally no one really cares where it *goes*.

And because of this; i.e.; the result of this; is that which is described in verses 44 and 45: "*Then he saith, I will return into my house from whence I came out; and when he is come, he findeth it empty, swept, and garnished. Then goeth he, and taketh with himself seven other spirits more wicked than himself, and they enter in and dwell there: and the last state of that man is worse than the first.*"

But with regard to Legion, it was where he was *to be sent*; i.e.; the *future* "location" that was Legion's concern. Legion believed that it was not going to be permitted to: "*walketh through dry places, seeking rest, and findeth none*;" and then to simply: "*enter in and dwell there*."

Instead Legion believed that he was to be *sent to abussŏs*; or: "*depthless*, i.e. (spec.) (infernal) "*abyss*," (Luke); or *chōra*: "through the idea of empty expanse," (Mark). And it was this fact, which was the cause for Legion's concerns regarding "*torment*."

Earlier it was stated that these words were changed because of *fear*. And one fear, is the fear that "unclean spirits" have; that man will discover the "unclean spirit's fear of being sent to the *abussŏs*.

Is this *abussŏs*, the same as the *abussŏs phrĕar*, or "*bottomless pit*" referenced in Revelation? This cannot be answered. But what is known is that "unclean spirits" fear being sent to that which is *abussŏs*; and they believe that there is "*torment*" for them therein.

What appears to be the same story, appears in Matthew 8:28-32:

"And when he was come to the other
side into the country of the Gergesenes,
there met him two possessed with devils,
coming out of the tombs, exceeding fierce,
so that no man might pass by that way.

And, behold, they cried out, saying,
What have we to do with thee,
Jesus, thou Son of God?
art thou come hither to torment
us before the time?

And there was a good way off from
them an herd of many swine feeding.

So the devils besought him, saying,
If thou cast us out, suffer us to go
away into the herd of swine.

And he said unto them, Go.

And when they were come out,
they went into the herd of swine:
and, behold, the whole herd of swine
ran violently down a steep place into
the sea, and perished in the waters."[6.12]

Here in Matthew, neither "choked," nor "drowned" appears. Instead we are told that the swine "*perished*" [The other discrepancies between these two "versions" are worthy of note.]

The original Greek word translated as "perished" is:

> "599 apŏthnēskō; from 575 and 2348; to *die* off (lit. or fig): - be dead, death, die, lie a-dying, be slain (x with)."[6.13]

Who is it that has the authority to not merely cause an "unclean spirit" to *ĕxĕrchŏmai*, or depart a man; but to also send it to *abussŏs*?

Luke 10:17-20 (KJV) tells us:

"Then the seventy returned with joy,
saying, "Lord, even the demons are
subject to us in Your name."

And He said to them, "I saw Satan fall
Like lightning from heaven.

Behold, I give you the authority to
trample on serpents and scorpions,

and over all the power of the enemy,
and nothing shall by any means hurt you.

Nevertheless do not rejoice in this,
that the spirits are subject to you,
but rather rejoice because
your names are written in heaven."""[6.14]

And there is something else going on in this story, something that the "upper echelon" of "unclean spirits" also fear; and perhaps fear even more than the *abussŏs.*

It must be remembered that after Jesus had "*commanded*" Legion to "*come out of the man,*" Legion did and said something very interesting: "*he cried out, and fell down before him, and with a loud voice said, What have I to do with thee, Jesus, thou Son of God most high? I beseech thee, torment me not.*"

Romans 10:13 (KJV) tells us:

"*For whosoever shall call upon the name*
of the Lord shall be saved."[6.15]

Acts 2:21 (KJV) tells us:

"*And it shall come to pass,*
that whosoever shall call on the name
of the Lord shall be saved."[6.16]

John 3:16 (KJV) tells us:

"For God so loved the world,
that he gave his only begotten Son,
that whosoever believeth
in him should not perish,
but have everlasting life."[6.17]

Romans 10:9 (KJV) tells us:

"That if thou shalt confess with thy
mouth the Lord Jesus, and shalt believe in
thine heart that God hath raised him from
the dead, thou shalt be saved."[6.18]

So here we are told how to be saved. Twice we are told: "*call upon the name of the Lord;*" once: "*believeth in him;*" and once: "*confess with thy mouth the Lord Jesus, and shalt believe in thine heart that God hath raised him from the dead.*"

And with regard to Legion: "*he cried out, and fell down before him, and with a loud voice said, What have I to do with thee, Jesus, thou Son of God most high? I beseech thee, torment me not.*"

Of course the last part of Romans 10:9, the: "*believe in thine heart that God hath raised him from the dead;*" was not possible for anyone; including Legion, at the time Jesus was physically alive.

Thus the question becomes whether or not this could actually be a story about a group of "*unclean* spirits," or "*devils,*" who were saved? To determine if this is so, examining what Jesus actually did afterward would be revealing.

After Legion had begged, ("*beseech*"); that Jesus not "*torment*" him; and told Jesus his (their) name; and begged, ("*besought*"), that Jesus would not command them to go to the *abussŏs*, (Luke); or *chōra*, (Mark); something unusual happened.

There was a herd of swine nearby, so Legion begged, ("*besought*"); Jesus to permit, ("*suffer*"), them, (the "*unclean spirits*"); to enter the swine, in lieu of commanding them to the "*torment*" of the *abussŏs*. Jesus in fact then permitted, ("*suffered*") them to do this.

And the result was: "*Then went the devils out of the man, and entered into the swine: and the herd ran violently down a steep place into the lake, and were choked.*" So the "*unclean spirits,*" entered the "unclean animals;" who then "*were choked.*" [It must be noted that "*unclean spirits*" being in a "*lake;*" seems to represent an entirely different situation than the "*unclean spirits*" that: "*walketh through dry places, seeking rest, and findeth none;*" as per the above Matthew 12:43.]

If these swine being "choked," (originally translated as "drowned"),[6.19] means *killed* here in Luke, as *apŏthnēskō* or "*perished*" in Matthew; then precisely what was it that happened to all of those "*unclean spirits*?"

We know that they were longer in the "*man.*" We know that they were not in the "*swine*"—

assuming all the swine were dead. We know they were not in the *abussŏs*, (Luke); or *chōra*, (Mark). And we know that they were not in *heaven*, as Jesus was still physically alive; and thus no sinner could get into heaven at that time.

This leaves only two possibilities. They either went to the *general* area of hell, which makes no degree of contextual sense; or they went to the *kŏlpŏs*; AKA: the Limbus Patrum, Bosom of Abraham. Those in the *kŏlpŏs*, are or were there awaiting the *availability* of salvation.

It is the possibility of *salvation* for "*unclean spirits*," that the "upper echelon" of "*unclean spirits*" also fear—perhaps even more than they fear the "*torment*" of the *abussŏs*?

With regard to Biblical *deletions*, it is a rather difficult task to determine precisely what it is that is *missing* from the Bible.

This is further compounded by the simple fact, that no one knows how many books are supposed to be contained in that which is considered to be: "The Bible." The "King James Version," is reputed to be the result of a compromise between the "clergy," who wanted none of the Bible released to the public; and King James, who wanted "full disclosure." Thus we are left with the "Apocrypha," roughly: "hidden things." This "Apocrypha" represents the books whose authenticity, and applicability to be included as part of "The Bible," remain largely in dispute.

One of these is somewhat easy. The books of the *Maccabees* or *Machabees*, are likely to be authentic books of the Bible, but are not part of the KJV. Thus the KJV is left without the story of Hanukkah/Chanukah/Ḥanukah; AKA: The Festival of Lights; except perhaps for a brief reference made to it by Jesus. But the Catholics, who do *not* celebrate Hanukkah, nevertheless include these books in their Bible.

The purported "Book of Phillip," seems to have been discounted with respect to authenticity. But it remains unknown if other books, such as the "Book of Enoch;" should be included.

However given the fact that God created man for the reasons previously set forth, (at least according to God); there seems to be little information about the *origins* of the very enemy that man was brought into existence to battle.

If it is again stipulated that *evil* means against God's will, irrespective of the nature of the act; and *wicked* is concerned with the *nature* of the act; man knows not with respect to the *origins* of either. If God is considered as the "set" whence all that exists emanated; it must be asked precisely how could there be any "subset" of this "set" brought into existence against His will? How could anything be brought into existence both in *accordance* with His will, and *against* His will; at the very same time?

To be clear, it is not the origins of the *aggĕlŏs*, who engaged in the *planaō* that is the issue. It seems reasonable that these were brought into existence by God, just as were the *aggĕlŏs*, who never engaged in the *planaō*. It is the source of, or for *planaō* that is unknown.

This question leads to highly speculative theories. But the truth is that man does not know how the original enemy, the source of or for *planaō*, came into existence. And the Bible provides little information in this regard.

It is not known what information may have been removed from the Bible concerning this. But for the enemy, this likely would have been his first objective—even long before the Bible was committed to paper.

With regard to potential *additions* to the Bible—

> "There is a passage in Matthew that merits extremely serious consideration. Here in this similar but different *story* than Legion, (is not a *parable*); the disciples had attempted to cast a demon out of a boy, but were unsuccessful.
>
> "The boy's father then brought the boy to Jesus to cast out the demon, and He, (Jesus), was successful. The disciples then inquired of Jesus as to why it was that they had failed.
>
> "Following is Matthew 17:14-19 according to *The King James Version*:
>
> *"And when they were*
> *come to the multitude,*

There came to him a
certain man, kneeling
down to him, and saying,

Lord, have mercy on my
son: for he is lunatick,
and sore vexed: for
oft times he falleth into
the fire, and oft
into the water.

And I brought him
to thy disciples,
and they could
not cure him.

Then Jesus answered
and said, O faithless and
perverse generation,

how long shall I be with
you? how long shall I
suffer you? bring him
hither to me.

And Jesus rebuked the
devil; and he departed
out of him:
and the child was cured
from that very hour.

Then came the disciples
to Jesus apart,

and said, Why could not
we cast him out?"[WEIB17]

"Matthew 17 verses 20-22 (KJV), then tell us:

20 "*And Jesus said unto*
them, Because of your
unbelief; for verily
I say unto you, If
Ye have faith as a grain
Of mustard seed,ye shall
say unto this mountain,
Remove hence to
yonder place;and it shall
remove; and nothing
shall be impossible
unto you."[WEIB18]

→21 "*Howbeit this kind*
goeth not out
but by prayer
and fasting."[WEIB19]←

22 "*And while they*
Abode in Galilee,
Jesus said unto them,
'The Son of man shall be
betrayed into the hands
of men:'"[WEIB20]

"The word "howbeit," which appears in verse 21; is not equivalent to: "How be it?" which would then represent a *question*.

"Rather; "howbeit" generally means "however;" representing a *statement* such as "nevertheless." This "nevertheless" represents an attempt to modify what was just stated rule in verse 20, for this particular situation. Thus this is represented as Jesus *answering* a question, and not the disciples *asking* another question.

"Verse 20 has to do with that which is immaterial; here unbelief, and as will be seen is sometimes also translated as insufficient "faith."

"But the inclusion of verse 21 completely negates what Jesus just stated in the preceding verse regarding unbelief or insufficient faith being *causative*; by stating in 21: "(nevertheless) *this kind not goeth out but by prayer and fasting*." The "but" here could also be reasonably translated as "except."

"It seems peculiar that Jesus would answer the disciples' question as He did in verse 20; and then in the very next verse tell them that all He just said in the previous verse did not apply in this case.

"And this is especially odd, because the original question He was asked was about this specific matter. So as it reads, Jesus must then have first answered a question about something else entirely different; and then went on to answer the question he was actually asked, negating what He had just said about other matters of which He was not asked.

"In addition, there is the matter of lack of specificity. In verse 20, Jesus speaks of the relative *quantities* of a "*mustard seed*," (cause); and a moving mountain, (effect). Yet; there is no mention in verse 21 of how much praying, or how much fasting is required.

"And it is clear that verse 22 begins an entirely different matter that is unrelated to
that which precedes it.

"Following is Matthew 17:20-22; but here according to the *New American Standard Bible*:

20 "*And He said unto them, "Because of the littleness of your faith; for truly I say to you,*

if you have faith the size
of a mustard seed,you
will say to this mountain,
"Move from here to
there," and it will move;
and nothing will be
impossible to you."[WEIB21]

→21 ["*But this kind does*
not go out
except by prayer
and fasting."][WEIB22]←

22 *And while they were*
gathering together in
Galilee Jesus said to
them, 'The Son of Man
is going to be delivered
into the hands of
men;'"[WEIB23]

"The most notable difference here in the NAS version, is the inclusion of *brackets*. According to NAS: "[] = In text, brackets indicate words probably not in the original writings."[WEIB24]

"So although clearly this passage appears in the KJV; it is likewise included in the NAS, but with the caveat that it is "probably not in the original writings."

"But given the presence of verse 21 in each of these two popular "versions," surely it must have come from somewhere. It seems that although it is not known whence verse 21 came, it is known whence it did not—the original writings, at least according to NAS.

"This leaves only writings that are *not original* as any possible source. It must also be remembered that this is a *story*, and these passages represent an eyewitness account.

"Following is Matthew 17:20-22; but here according to the *New International Version Bible*:

20 "*He replied, "Because*
you so little faith.
I tell you the truth, if you
Have faith as small as a
mustard seed, you can
say to this mountain,
'Move from here to
there' and it will move
."Nothing will be
impossible for you."[WEIB25]

→21 (No verse is
present—
nothing.)[WEIB26]←

22 "When they came
together Galilee,
he said to them,
'The Son of Man
is going to be betrayed
into the hands of
*men.'"*WEIB27

"Much like the "thirteenth floor" on many buildings; here in the NIV, there is no 21st verse present in Matthew 17. Matthew 17 simply goes from verse 20, to verse 22; with no verse 21.

"The difference here is that many buildings in fact do actually have a thirteenth floor; it is just called something else—meaning that there is the actuality of a floor 13 stories up, it is just *called* something different.

"But here in Matthew, it is *not* a matter of these words existing, and merely a difference of opinion as to where they appear, or what they are numbered. Rather, there is disagreement as to whether or not Jesus actually ever spoke these words. Thus the existence of this very actuality itself is in question.

"It should be asked precisely who or what non-"original" source would have added verse 21; and for what specific reason(s)?

"Although it is not possible to ascertain the particular *source* of this particular "verse;" nevertheless, (*howbeit*), some *reasons* for this "addition" can be logically derived.

"In verse 20, it is clear that Jesus is speaking of *belief* or *faith* that provides the means by which this enemy is cast out. This means that the source of this power is *the individual* that is directly involved in the casting out.

"It is the *will* of the individual, along with *faith* that provides the F; and the MA is the subsequent exit of the demon; with the M here being considered as the demon, and the A the movement out.

"But if verse 21 were true, then this would mean that a tiny force that is capable of moving a mountain; would somehow nevertheless be insufficient for casting out a demon.

"And more importantly; here in verse 21, the source of the power becomes *indirect*.

"Meaning; that here it is no longer the will of the individual along with faith that *directly* provides the actuality of F, and the subsequent MA of the exit of the demon.

"Instead; this "fasting" and "prayer" merely provide an immaterial imbalance, (*potential*); which is then, (hopefully), balanced by God; by *Him* providing the F and subsequent MA causing the exit, (*kinetic*), of the demon.

"The hierarchy is God, man, and then all else. This "all else" includes angels and demons. Angels must obey man's will, unless man's will conflicts with God's will. When man's will and God's will conflict; God's will necessarily prevails.

"Since a fair argument exists that demons are or were actually angels, the same rule applies. Whenever a human is possessed by a demon, this is not God's will. But unfortunately, this is much more complex than it seems.

"Up to a certain point, just as was the case with the *attacks* on Job; demonic *possession* is also often possible, because of the previous actions of the "host."

"This *possession*, is part of the balancing of the actuality of the host's free will from previous willful actions. Simply because this may not be a part of any given host's *reality* regarding any given willful action, this in no way means it is not so. In these cases, it is merely another part of the *actuality* of the totality of the action. [See Monograph #602 "*It's Not Just a Theory*" for a study of this process.]

"It is not God's will that any man be in the condition of demonic possession. But demonic possession can be the *secondary* result of man willfully disobeying God's will.

"Thus it is the violation of God's will *by* man; which then results in a condition that is not God's will *for* man. In the case of Job, this was permission for the enemy to *attack*, (but not possess or kill), Job. In the case of possession; although the magnitudes may be different; the balancing *process* is nevertheless quite similar.

"So *if* there is a verse 21, or perhaps better stated if verse 21 is an actuality; it seems that there are then *two* ways presented to cast out a demon.

"One is *direct* and based upon the force created both by the will and the faith or belief of man, consistent with that which Jesus spoke in verse 20.

"The other, is the creation of an immaterial imbalance by praying and fasting. This would represent an *indirect* action; as this force is not "directly directed" at the demon, which is the purported reason for verse 21.

"What the question here *is not*; is whether the creation of a sufficient immaterial imbalance can sometimes provide God with sufficient "license" to cast out a demon, as this can happen.

"Why license? Because if license were not required, and possession is against God's will; why then does He not just do it Himself without any "prayer and fasting?"

"The answer is that He cannot do this without simultaneously *violating* His own laws. Man had previously been given this authority in Genesis 1:28. Thus for God to do this directly *Himself*, an immaterial imbalance created by man's will in prayer and fasting is required, in order to "pay" for;" i.e.; *balance*; this action on the part of God.

"What the question here actually *is*; is whether or not Jesus made this statement in response to the inquiry as to why the disciples failed. The clear and convincing evidence is that He did not.

"Thus with verse 21 removed, it was not the absence of prayer and fasting that caused, or even had anything to do with this failure of the disciples attempts. But rather, it was insufficient *faith*—just as Jesus stated in the verse, (verse 20), immediately preceding verse 21..."[6.20] [Excerpt from "*Wisdom Essentials - Inevitable*

Balance." Reprinted by Permission]

A word of caution is necessary. "Unclean spirits" are subject to the will of man. However potential serious dangers lie in any confrontation with any "unclean spirit." This is not an issue of man's *authority*, but rather an issue of their knowledge and experience—"unclean spirits" too learn by observation.

These entities have been *lying* to mankind; and attempting to *manipulate* mankind, (and other life forms); for hundreds of millennia—and with a surprisingly high degree of success. Any neophyte attempting to confront these entities is potentially placing themselves in danger because of this.

The "phantom verse" Matthew 17:21, is one example of attempting to change the dynamics of the situation. Man has the authority, and "unclean spirits" cannot change this. But what they can change, is man's *reality* of this authority; thereby hoping to achieve the same result.

Most neophytes to this process will act out of anger. This is unwise, as this anger clouds one's judgment, and provides a foothold for the enemy.

Many neophytes will begin by starting a "conversation"—generally beginning with: "What is your name?" This is also quite unwise, as this provides openings for attacks; hoping at minimum to delay action, and cause doubt. And it must be asked if "unclean spirits" represent a reliable source of truth when answering any question, or providing any information?

And even many "professionals," employ much

mummery and flummery; and then *importune* God to do that which man was given clear authority to do.

When undertaking any endeavor, one must first obtain sufficient knowledge—not only in order to succeed; but to not end up with a situation worse than that which with one began.

Acts 19:13-16 (KJV) tells us:

"Then certain of the vagabond
Jews, exorcists,
took upon them to call over them
which had evil spirits the name o
f the Lord Jesus, saying,
We adjure you by Jesus
whom Paul preacheth.

And there were seven
sons of one Sceva,
a Jew, and chief of the priests,
which did so.

And the evil spirit answered and said,
Jesus I know, and Paul I know;
but who are ye?

And the man in whom the
evil spirit was leaped on them,
and overcame them,
and prevailed against them,
so that they fled out of that
house naked and wounded."[6.21]

7

The Means to the End

Earlier, Genesis 1:28 was cited as God's instruction to man: "*And God blessed them, and God said unto them, Be fruitful, and multiply, and replenish the earth, and subdue it: and have dominion over the fish of the sea, and over the fowl of the air, and over every living thing that moveth upon the earth.*"

And again, the "*subdue it*" part is: "kâbash; a prim. root; to *tread* down; hence neg. to *disregard*; pos. to *conquer, subjugate, violate*: - bring into bondage, force, keep under, subdue, bring into subjection." The English word *kibosh* is derived from *kâbash*.

And although man translates what God Himself called man as "*host*;" the actual word provided by Moses, (assuming *Mosaic* authorship of Genesis), again is: "6635 tsâbâ' or ts^{e}bâ'âh from 6633; a *mass* of persons (or fig. things), espec. reg. organized for war (an *army*); by impl. a *campaign*, lit. or fig. (spec. *hardship, worship*): -appointed time, (+) army, (+) battle, company, host, service, soldiers, waiting upon, war (fare)."

So we are told that it is the purpose of man acting as *tsâbâ'*, or: "a *mass* of persons (or fig. things), espec. reg. organized for war;" to kâbash, or: "to *tread* down... to *conquer, subjugate, violate*: -bring into bondage, force, keep under, subdue, bring into subjection;" the earth—at least according to what God said.

But these are very *general* instructions, much more like the *goal* of or for mankind; rather than "host specific," which is the case with *objectives*. *Objectives* are considered as *SMART*; with this acronym here meaning: Specific, Measurable, Achievable, Realistic, and Time sensitive.

Thus although here God told us the purpose of mankind in the *general* sense; precisely what the purpose of each *individual* should ideally be, cannot be derived from these words. Neither are we told here precisely *how*; i.e.; *by what means*, we are each to play our unique roles.

"Ephesians 6:17 tells us:

"And take the helmet

*of salvation, and
the sword of the Spirit,
which is the word of
God:*"WENJAT24

"Tucked in at the very end of the list of defensive, (increasing resistance), measures in the preceding verses, and ending here in verse 17 after the last "and;" something rather interesting appears. In fact; therein lies a "bomb." And it is a rather interesting and quite powerful "bomb;"—the same representing the provision of a key instruction: "*(take) the sword of the Spirit, which is the word of God.*"

"This instruction is the only *offensive* (voltage lowering) instruction given in these verses.

"What does *"(take) the sword of the Spirit, which is the word of God" mean*?

"The actual original Greek word translated as "sword" is:

> "3162 machaira; prob. fem. of a presumed der. of *3163*; a *knife*, i.e. *dirk*; fig. *war*, judicial *punishment*: - sword."WENJAT25

"As can be seen, the translation as "sword" is misleading. A dirk is not a sword. "Knife" or "Dagger" would be a better translation. These are designed for "up close and personal" combat. This is important because this (close up and tailor made), is precisely how the enemy attacks.

"The figurative meaning should also be noted, that of "judicial punishment." There is an old saying: "Don't stick your head in the boxing ring if you don't want to get punched." It is the enemy who chooses to institute an attack. If the result is encountering a counterattack with a dirk, and he/it leaves a bit "bloodied," then he or it deserved it. But again, this should never be combined with anything that is of the enemy such as anger, hatred, etc. It is justice; ("judicial punishment"), and not vengeance that should be sought. If that which is of the enemy is at any time utilized, this can then easily be utilized by the enemy as a foothold.

"The actual Greek word translated as "spirit" is:

> "*4151* pnĕuma; from *4154*; a *current* of air, i.e. *breath* (*blast*) or a *breeze*; by anal. or fig. a *spirit*, i.e. (human) the rational *soul*, (by impl.) *vital principle*,

> mental *disposition* etc..."[WENJAT26]

"Thus; "the knife of the soul" is a better translation. And precisely what is this "knife of the soul?"

"It is the "word of God." What is this word? The actual Greek "word" translated here as "word" is:

> "*4487* rhēma; from *4483*; an *utterance* (individ., collect. or spec.); by impl. a *matter* or *topic* (espec. of narration, command or dispute); with a neg. *naught* whatever..."[WENJAT27]

"John 1:1 tells us:

> "*In the beginning was the Word, and the Word was with God, and the Word was God.*"[WENJAT28]

"However the actual word translated here three times as "Word" is not rhēma, but rather:

> "*3056* lŏgŏs; from *3004*; something *said* (including

> the *thought*); by impl. a *topic* (subject of discourse), also *reasoning* (the mental faculty) or *motive*; by extens. a *computation*; spec. (with the art. In John) the Divine *Expression* (i.e. *Christ*)"[WENJAT29]

> "So it must be asked what is the difference between rhēma and lŏgŏs; and why was rhēma used by Paul, and lŏgŏs used in John?
>
> "Paul was giving instructions for *future* behavior, and John was recollecting *past* events. Thus rhēma; meaning an *utterance*; refers to what God *is* or *will be* saying "real time." Lŏgŏs refers to what God *has* or *had already* said."[7.1] [Excerpt from "*Wisdom Essentials - Its Not Just A Theory*,"]

If one goes to the *lŏgŏs*, or the written word of God; and then also receives *rhēma*, or the "real time" "utterance" word of God; this is often referred to as *Bibliomancy*.

How is it that God provides this *rhēma*? Does He actually speak out loud? Not usually—although He has on occasion. God is usually much more subtle than this.

God will provide *rhēma* in a variety of ways: "I just had an idea." "I just had a feeling." "Something just told me to." "Somehow I just knew;" are all examples of the acknowledgement of the *actual* receipt of *rhēma*—whether this is *realized* or not.

There exists some basic or foundational *lŏgŏs*, originally presented as *rhēma*; and these are generally referred to as: "The Commandments." This is a bit of a misnomer, as God never actually "commanded" us to obey them—at least when they appear in Exodus 20. Instead, he asked us to do what is generally translated as "keep" them.

When God the Father spoke about "keeping" His "Commandments," the original Hebrew word is:

> "8104: shâmar; A prim. root; prop. to *hedge* about (as with thorns), i.e. *guard*; gen. to *protect*, *attend to*, etc.: - beware, be circumspect, take heed (to self), keep (-er, self), mark, look narrowly, observe, preserve, regard, reserve, save (self), sure, (that lay) wait (for), watch (-man)."[7.2]

And when Jesus spoke about "keeping" his "Commandments," the original Greek word is:

> "5083 tērĕō; from tĕrŏs (a *watch*; perh. akin to 2334); to *guard* (from *loss* or *injury*, prop. by keeping *the eye* upon..."[7.3]

Thus the "Commandments" are actually *informational* in nature; and not meant to represent an actual "command," in the sense of *requiring* obedience—at least according to the words chosen by God the Father, and Jesus.

The free will of man is so important, that even God himself would not interfere with man's decision to obey or not obey these commandments; but only "requires" that we *shâmar* or *tērĕō* the information; and then use this information in the decision making process. But these "Commandments" are the same for all, no matter what specific role any given host was designed to play.

Why is it that man should choose to obey these "Commandments?" The answer depends upon precisely what it is that one wants to subsequently reap. "Sowing" and "reaping" are not separate actualities. Whatever one chooses to "sow," represents a part of one actuality; with the ultimate and unavoidable "reaping" representing the other part of this *very same actuality*, resulting in balance.

Putting the *kibosh*, on the earth; or as God actually stated in Genesis 1:28 via the Hebrew *kâbash*; is again very broad, or *goal* oriented. Again, although most Bible "experts" would agree that the Bible is a "book about redemption;" they do *not* agree that it is the redemption of the earth to which this "book about redemption" characterization refers. They do not understand that the original *created* hosts were brought into existence to *kâbash* the *earth*; and then much later the *formation* of the man known as Adam was the first act in the redemption of the *hosts*—to redeem the redeemers.

It is a "pretty tough sell," to suggest that the fruits of God's efforts as stated in Genesis 1:27: "*So God created man in his own image, in the image of God created he him; male and female created he them;*" required redemption from the "get go." It was because of the *contamination* of the *created* hosts from contact with the enemy while knowingly or unknowingly engaged in the *kâbash* process; that necessitated the beginning of the redemptive process for man. This process began with the *formation* of the "first Adam;" and was "finished" by the "last Adam."

This is why considering redemption of man as literal *grace*, is not true. *Grace* is that which is undeserved, or a "free gift." [The tautological nature of "free gift" is duly noted.] The provision of the redemption of man; i.e.; man's *salvation*; is not *grace* but rather a *gratuity*.

Ephesians 2:8 (KJV) tells us:

> *"For by grace are ye*
> *saved through faith;*
> *and that not of yourselves:*
> *it is the gift of God:"*[7.4]

The original Greek word translated as "grace" is:

> "5485 charis; from 5463; *graciousness* (as *gratifying*), of manner or act (abstr. or concr.; lit., fig. or spiritual; espec. the divine influence upon the heart, and its reflection in the life; including *gratitude*)..."[7.5]

> "5463 chairō; a prim. verb; to *be "cheer" ful*, i.e. calmly *happy* or well-off; impers. espec. as salutation (on meeting or parting), *be well*: - farewell, be glad, Godspeed, greeting, hail, joy(-fully), rejoice."[7.6]

The emphases on "as gratifying," and "including *gratitude*;" in the definition of *charis*, should not be overlooked.

And based upon the definition of the purported root of *charis*, (chairō); and because of the added "i;" it seems that what is listed as the root of *charis*, "from 5463" which is *chairō*; there seems to be a typographical error. What is listed as the root of *charis*, should likely be listed as: "from 5483;" and not: "from 5463."

> "5483 charizŏmai; mid. from 5485; to grant as a *favor* i.e. gratuitously, in kindness, pardon or rescue: - deliver, (frankly) forgive, (freely) give, grant."[7.7]

And another Greek word related to *charis* is:

> "5486 charisma; from 5483; a (divine) *gratuity*, i.e. *deliverance* (from danger or passion); (spec.) a (spiritual) *endowment*, i.e. (subj.) religious *qualification* or obj.) miraculous *faculty*: - (free) gift."[7.8]

As can be seen, *charisma* is also from 5483 *charizŏmai*. In each of these words, some form of *gratitude* or *gratuity* is referenced.

This is unlike the Greek word translated in this same passage as "gift," which is:

> "1435 dōrŏn; a *present*; spec. a *sacrifice*: - gift, offering."[7.9]

It is *dōrŏn* that is translated as the "*gifts*" to Jesus from the Magi, in Matthew 2:11 (KJV).[7.10] Thus *dōrŏn*; (unlike "1431 dōrĕa; from *1435*; a *gratuity*: - gift");[7.11] refers to a *gift*, which if truly a (free) gift; is more like grace—albeit requiring: "spec. a *sacrifice*," presumably on the part of the "giver."

But the *charis* "family of words;" refers not to *grace*, or any *undeserved* gift; but rather refer to a *gratitude* or a *gratuity* in some form or another.

Why does this matter?

As previously stated, literal "grace;" is getting something of *positive* value that one *does not* deserve. And its counterpart, "mercy;" is *not* getting something of *negative* value one in fact *does* deserve.

An actual or true, (the "*free*"), gift, is literal *grace*; in that it is or was not deserved, because it was not paid for in any way or manner. Thus this is something of positive value that is undeserved

But any type of *gratuity* is in fact *deserved* in some way or manner; and thus not any type of *gift*, unless it vastly exceeds that which would normally be expected. And even then, there would then actually exist both a *gratuity*, and a *gift*.

So the deserved *gratuity*, or the correct meaning of the *charis* "family of words," in the case of *salvation*; is because of the impossible position man is in. God, who is *omniscient*, knew way ahead of time that there was no way any man, (except Himself); could ever win every battle with the enemy—particularly when often man does not even know he is involved in a war, or what the rules are. And because of the unfairness of this situation, this requires a gratuity.

One may argue that the formation of the first Adam took way too long, as this event occurred less than ten thousand years ago. But God has to play by the rules, and is subject to delay by man's errors. Thus the *kŏlpŏs*, or Bosom of Abraham, or Limbus Patrum, (the: "air conditioned section of hell"); was established for those who physically died prior to the availability of salvation.

But *redeem* and *subdue* are not necessarily the same. To simply "*subdue*," "put the kibosh on," or *kâbash*; does not necessarily mean redemption. These very same acts could be evil, wicked, or both. Whether or not it is a redemptive act; depends upon other factors.

Each human being is and was designed and brought into existence with specific tasks in mind.

One way to find out what these are; is the above *lŏgŏs*, or the written word of God; and *rhēma*. These are largely *informational* in nature.

At the time of that which is commonly known as: "The Last Supper," arguably: "The Last Seder," for Christians; Jesus said something very interesting. And this statement is the subject of controversy even today.

John 14:12 (KJV) tells us:

"*Verily, verily, I say unto you,*
He that believeth on me,
the works that I do shall he do also;
and greater works than
these shall he do;
because I go unto my Father."[7.12]

The actual Greek word translated as "works" both times is:

> "2041 ĕrgŏn; from a prim. (but obsol.) ĕrgō (to *work*); *toil* (as an effort or occupation); by impl. an *act*: - deed, doing, labour, work."[7.13]

The original Greek word translated here as "greater" is:

> "3187 mĕizōn; irreg. compar. of 3173; *larger* (lit. or fig., spec. in age): - elder, greater (-est), more."[7.14]

Here "*works*" used in this context, is generally considered to represent the *results* or *fruits*. But the above definition of *ĕrgŏn* is unclear, as to whether this also represents the action of working as well.

Today an *erg* is: "a centimeter-gram-second unit of work equal to the work done by a force of one dyne acting through a distance of one centimeter and equivalent to 10^{-7} joule."[7.15]

The use of the term *ergonomics*, particularly by furniture manufacturers, is commonplace today.

But either way, we are being told that *if* the conditions of this statement are met; *then* greater or *mĕizōn* results than even those that Jesus achieved can be accomplished, after He went to the "Father."

If *ĕrgŏn* is translated as "*works*" is considered a *noun*; then greater *results* are possible. If *ĕrgŏn* is translated as "*works*" is considered a *verb*; then greater *means* are possible.

This passage is silent about the "type of means," and thus the "type of results;" to which this passage refers. Here "type of," refers to whether or not the *means* and/or *results* are consistent with, or inconsistent with natural law.

There are two types of *power* or *means* available in the universe:

> *dynamikós*: (G) natural power, "from Greek *dynamikós* powerful, from *dynamis* power, from *dynasthai* be able, have power;"[7.16]

> *dunamis*: (G) supernatural power "*1411* dunamis; from *1410*; *force* (lit. or fig.); spec. miraculous *power* (usually by impl. a *miracle* itself)..."[7.17]

So it must be asked precisely which power it is to which Jesus is referring that will result in greater, or *mĕizōn*; "*works*," or *ĕrgŏn*? Is it *dynamikós*, or *natural* power, that will result in greater *natural* results; or is it *dunamis*, or *supernatural* power, that will result in greater *supernatural* results, (miracles); to which Jesus is referring?

Before this is addressed, the enemy has been quite busy trying to change the meaning of this passage. This alone should reveal which power it is to which Jesus is referring. There are two main methods by which the enemy has been attempting to change the meaning of this passage:

The *first* way, is the: "Apostolic Era Only" view of *dunamis*. Here it is proffered that *dunamis* was available in this "Apostolic" Era," but is no longer available today. There is no scriptural basis for this "view." But it is much easier for those who have no *dunamis*, to blame it on *unavailability*, rather than their *inability*—and this display of hubris pleases the enemy greatly.

And the *second* way, is to tacitly insert the words: "number of," or "numbers of;" in between *mĕizōn* and *ĕrgŏn*. So "greater number of works" or "greater numbers of works" becomes the new translation. The "rationale" for this, is that since there are more Christians today, a greater number of works is or are possible. Of course this is nonsense, as *mĕizōn* is adjectivally describing *ĕrgŏn*; and the word number does not appear anywhere in the passage. And it is unclear if this "view" includes *dunamis*; or refers to *dynamikós* only.

Jesus was known for His *supernatural* or *dunamic* abilities, among many other things; rather than any *natural* or *dynamic* abilities. And contextually, *dunamis* fits quite well; while *dynamikós* would not.

But to understand *dunamis*, it must first be understood that it does not occur alone—even if its counterpart occurs *before* or *after* the *dunamis*.

In order to understand the Greek *dunamis*, the examination of a certain Hebrew word would be beneficial:

> "4853 massâ' from 5375; a burden; spec. tribute, or (abstr.) porterage; fig. an utterance, chiefly a doom, espec. singing; mental desire: - burden, carry away, prophesy..."[7.18]

Here with the Hebrew *massâ'*, it can be seen that translations of *massâ'* can be "prophesy" or "burden;" i.e.; supernatural power; or *personal*, or *subjective* "weight." This is because they always come together as a unit, even if there is a time lag. Here the Hebrew word *massâ'*, represents both, and as can be seen, is translated either way.

So what is it that is this counterpart of *dunamis*? The answer of course is *talent*—but not *talent* as commonly understood.

As *commonly* understood, *talent* might even be the very *dunamis* itself. Someone who has *talent*, usually has some type of capabilities in excess of those commonly seen. These unusual capabilities may be *dunamic* in nature; but are often called either *talent*, or *a gift*. With respect to the subject under discussion however; these capabilities are in fact neither *talent*, nor a *gift*.

Although a detailed analysis of this is beyond the scope of this work; the: "Talent Man Story," (actually a parable); is the explanation of the relationship between *talent* and *dunamis*. [See Chapter 10, "*True Talent*," contained in: "*Alleged Fantasy, Volume I Foundations*;" for this detailed analysis.]

So what is this *talent*? Many believe that a *talent* is a Hebrew unit of measure, ranging from 80 to 120 pounds, depending upon whether *common* or *royal*. But the truth is that *talent* actually is from the Greek:

> "5007 talantŏn; neut. of a presumed der. of the orig. form of tiaō (to *bear*; equiv. to 5342); a *balance* (as *supporting* weights), i.e. (by impl.) a certain *weight* (and thence a *coin* or rather *sum* of money) or "*talent*": - talent."[7.19]

> "5342 phĕrō; a prim. verb... to "*bear*" or *carry*."[7.20]

As can be seen, *talantŏn*; and its equivalent *phĕrō*; are concerned with *subjective* weight; and the actions: "bear," "carry," and "balance." Thus it is the *effect* of this weight upon the one bearing or carrying this weight; and not the actual *objective* weight with which *talantŏn* is concerned.

The *implied* definition of *talantŏn* as: "a certain *weight* (and thence a *coin* or rather *sum* of money)," refers to the *reliability* of the amount of weight; and not any particular *objective* amount of weight.

In the aforementioned "Talent Man" parable, each was given *talantŏn* in accordance with the amount of *dunamis*, (not *dynamikós*), they each possessed. Two of the three worked, (put ergs into), their *talantŏn*; and received more. One buried his talent, and it was taken from him. This parable describes a *process*.

Unlike *lŏgŏs*, or the written word of God; or *rhēma*, or the "real time" word of God, which are largely informational; *talantŏn* is more *emotional* in nature. But it is not *emotional* in the usual sense.

A distinction must be made here between *feelings* and *emotions*. For these discussions, *feelings* represent the acquisition of information without the use of normal five senses. "I just knew I should," and "Something just told me to;" would thus be reasonably equivalent by this definition of *feelings*.

But *emotions* are entirely different. *Emotion* contains the root "motion;" thus implying an *imbalanced* state. How is this imbalanced state balanced? The answer is motion; with "move out" representing a fair definition of *e-motion*.

A *talantŏn* is an emotional imbalance that is caused by God, in furtherance of a specific reaction, by a specific host; to do some specific thing God wants done; i.e.; *motivation* to do something. Unlike "normal" emotions, a *talantŏn* will not dissipate in the short term; although a *talantŏn* can be "buried;" i.e.; ignored and will eventually dissipate.

And also unlike most "normal" emotions, with a *talantŏn*; one will have "no peace" unless and until there is appropriate motion. And again, the *talantŏn* is the other side of the actuality known as *dunamis*. In Hebrew one word, massâ', describes the phenomenon—both the supernatural power, *and* the burden or weight. But in Greek, there are two words required to describe this phenomenon: *dunamis* for the supernatural power part; and *talantŏn* for the burden, or (balancing) weight.

How does one distinguish *dunamis*, from *dynamikós*? If it is a certainty; or perhaps better stated that to the extent that it is a certainty that any natural law was violated, then it is with this same degree of certainty, by definition *dunamis*.

And the reasonable read, is that Jesus Himself told us that if one meets the conditions in His statement, then that person would be capable of greater works than even Jesus did.

But as the "Talent Man" story tells us, this is a *process*. And every process must begin at some point. Where does this process begin for each of us?

Romans 12:3 (KJV) tells us:

"For I say, through the grace
given unto me,
to every man that is among you,
not to think of himself more
highly than he ought to think;
but to think soberly,
according as God hath dealt
to every man the measure of faith."[7.21]

"Precisely what is this: "*dealt to every man the measure of faith*?" Meaning, since this is proffered as the reason why one should not: "think more highly than he ought to think" about himself; precisely what is this that is under discussion.

"One answer to this is "seed *ĕxŏusia*," or baseline *dunamic* power and authority. This is the granting of say "one talent," in the hope of a host working this *talantŏn*; and obtaining at least one of the earlier coined *duna* of *dunamis* in return."[7.22]

Here the word "*faith*" is the aforementioned *pistis*,[7.23] meaning "persuade" or "convince." How is this done?

One way is to "see the system work," as explained in the "Talent Man" parable. Work the *talantŏn*, and get the *dunamis*; and then do it again when the next *talantŏn* arrives.

Another way is by the demonstration of this *dunamis* to others. The latter is precisely what Jesus did. Unbeknownst to most; many, (but not all), of the miracles performed by Jesus had been performed by others in the past. In addition to fulfilling the Biblical prophesy, this was done to remind people of their capabilities. In fact, it could be reasonably argued that providing this reminder was the very purpose for some of that which was included in these particular prophesies.

Rhēma and *lŏgŏs* are largely *informational*; but either can lead to the acquisition of *dunamis*. And it is the application of *ergs* into the system, which will increase the *dunamic* capabilities. The *talantŏn* provides the "drive," or the "insatiable" desire to move; and the application of ergs ultimately results in increased levels of *dunamis*. And this cycle can be repeated until: "*greater works than,*" "*the works that I do,*" "*shall he do.*" And since Jesus already went: "*unto my Father;*" this power is available right now to any: "*He that believeth on me, the works that I do.*"

Any host's acquisition of *dunamis*, or supernatural power, represents a serious *offensive* threat to the enemy. But the level of this *offensive* threat depends upon both the *level* of power acquired; and the *will* of the host. Thus the efficacy of this "*sword,*" or dirk; the *machaira* of the *pneuma*; is the result of the *understanding of*, and the *acting upon* the Word of God.

The enemy not only does not want any host to obtain *dunamis*; but he does not want any host to even know *dunamis* is even obtainable. And should any host become aware of *dunamic* capabilities, and then obtain any level of the same; it is *will* that is then severely attacked.

Matthew 7:13-14 (KJV) tells us:

> "*Enter ye in at the strait gate:*
> *for wide is the gate, and broad is the way,*
> *that leadeth to destruction,*
> *and many there be which go in thereat:*
>
> *Because strait is the gate,*
> *and narrow is the way,*
> *which leadeth unto life,*
> *and few there be that find it.*"[7.24]

Most believe that Jesus is speaking here of salvation; i.e.; these are the same "gates," as the "gates" in the passages of Luke 13:23-25. However as will shortly be seen, this is not so.

8

The Out Crowd

Luke 13:23-25 (KJV) tells us:

"Then said one unto him, Lord,
are there few that be saved?

And he said unto them,
Strive to enter in at the strait gate:
for many, I say unto you,
will seek to enter in,
and shall not be able.

When once the master of the
house is risen up,
and hath shut to the door,

and ye begin to stand without,
and to knock at the door, saying,
Lord, Lord, open unto us;
and he shall answer and say unto you,
I know you not whence ye are.'"[8.1]

"Here in Luke, it seems Jesus is clearly referring to salvation, as that was the subject of the inquiry to him: "*are there just a few who are being saved?*"

"The original Greek word translated as "saved" in Luke 13:23 is:

> "4982 sōzō; from a prim. sōs (contr. for obsol. saŏs "*safe*"); to *save*, i.e. *deliver* or *protect* (lit. or fig.): - heal, preserve, save (self), do well, be (make) whole."[AF5.12]

"...The *context* of Jesus' answer to the *question*; is critical in understanding the meaning of these passages. The *question* had to do with *how many* are being saved: "*are there few that be saved?*"

"Thus it seems reasonable that Jesus' *answer* would, at least in some way or manner, be concerned with this very same matter.

"The actual Greek word translated as "strait" here in Luke 13:24: "*Strive to enter in at the strait gate*," is:

> "4728 stĕnŏs; prob, from the base of *2476*; *narrow* (from obstacles *standing* close about): - strait."[AF5.13]

"Here there is a sense of "narrow" or a "strait," as it relates to the presence of *obstacles*. The common definition of *strait* is consistent with this, (see *stenosis*). But if "strait" is *spoken* instead of *read*, many would hear the word "straight," as in non-crooked, or the shortest distance between two points.

"The *struggle*, has to do with whether few or many will obtain salvation by entering the "*strait*" door, or via Jesus himself; as He is the only "door" to salvation. In fact, today there are many more obstacles causing a narrowing or an even "straiter strait." Much of this additional narrowing, is the direct result of governmental actions—most particularly the courts."[8.2]

But Matthew 7:13-14 (KJV) tells us:

*"Enter ye in at the strait gate:
for wide is the gate, and broad is
the way, that leadeth to destruction,
and many there be which go in thereat:*

*Because strait is the gate,
and narrow is the way,
which leadeth unto life,
and few there be that find it."*[8.3]

Once again, most believe that here in Matthew 7:13-14, Jesus is also speaking of *salvation*, as He was in the above passages in Luke 13:23-25; however—

> "At this juncture, in order to provide proper *context* for Matthew 7:13-14 above, it would be appropriate, arguably *necessary*, to consider the verses being those which *directly precede* the above Matthew: 7:13-14, namely Matthew 7:7-12.
>
> "It becomes obvious that the topic Jesus is speaking about here in these preceding verses, Matthew 7:7-12, is not *salvation*, but rather aspects of our *behavior*.
>
> "Matthew 7:7-12 (KJV) tells us:

*"Ask, and it shall be given you;
seek, and ye shall find; knock,*

and it shall be opened unto you:

For every one that asketh receiveth;
and he that seeketh findeth;
and to him that knocketh
it shall be opened.

Or what man is there of you,
whom if his son ask bread,
will he give him a stone?

Or if he ask a fish,
will he give him a serpent?
If ye then, being evil,
know how to give good gifts
unto your children,
how much more shall your Father
which is in heaven give good
things to them that ask him?

Therefore all things whatsoever
ye would that men should do to you,
do ye even so to them:
for this is the law
and the prophets."[AF5.4]

"Firstly, it must be determined precisely what the meaning of the two "its" are in verse 7: "*Ask, and it shall be given you,*" and: "*knock, and it shall be opened unto you;*" as well as the meaning of the singular "it" in verse 8:

"to him that knocketh it shall be opened;"—respectively.

"The *second* "it" in verse 7, ("*knock, and it shall be opened unto you*"); sounds suspiciously like the *salvation* door in Luke, which will be closed at some point in time.

"But the *first* "it" in verse 7, (*Ask, and it shall be given you*"); reads a bit differently. Here the "it" is something that will be given, and given in accord with whatever it was that was "asked for."

"Thus it seems that in order for this particular, (the *first*), "*it*" to be limited to something related to a *door*; it seems one would to have had to have *asked* for a door—assuming the "*knock*," "*knocketh*," and "*opened;*" refer to actions taken upon a door.

"The "*it*" in verse 8, ("*and to him that knocketh it shall be opened*"); is provided as part of an *explanation* of some type of principle, as we are told: "*For* (because) *every one that asketh receiveth; and he that seeketh findeth;*" appearing just before: "*and to him that knocketh it shall be opened.*"

"There are then some examples cited, and we are then provided with the conclusion beginning with a "*therefore;*" or what an attorney might phrase as: "For all of the foregoing

> reasons: "*Therefore*; ("For all of the foregoing reasons"); *all things whatsoever ye would that men should do to you, do ye even so to them: for this is the law and the prophets*."
>
> "This is Jesus explaining what is contemporarily referred to as the law of *karma*, or law *compensation*—no matter how angry some "Christian folk" may become by associating *Jesus*' teachings, with a word of *Buddhist* origin.
>
> "...Jesus concludes the subject of these passages with: "*for this is the law and the prophets*."[8.4]

After concluding these subjects, Jesus then begins speaking about an entirely different subject in the very next verses, the verses under analysis: Matthew 7:13-14.

Again, most believe this subject to be *salvation* in Matthew 7:13-14, just as in Luke 13:23-25; but careful

analysis proves this is not so.

Here again is Matthew 7:13-14 (KJV):

"Enter ye in at the strait gate:
for wide is the gate,
and broad is the way,
that leadeth to destruction,
and many there be which
go in thereat:

Because strait is the gate,
and narrow is the way,
which leadeth unto life,
and few there be that find it."

"The actual Greek word translated as "strait" in "*strait gate*" here in Matthew 7:13 is also *stĕnŏs.*[AF5.17]

"The actual Greek word translated as "gate," is as was seen previously in Luke:

> 4439 pulē; appar. a prim. word; a *gate*, i.e. the leaf or wing of a folding *entrance* (lit. or fig.): - gate."[AF5.18]

"The actual Greek word translated as "wide," is:

> "4116 platus; from *4111*; spread out "*flat*" ("plot"), i.e. *broad*: - wide."[AF5.19]

"The actual Greek word translated as "broad," is:

> "2149 ĕuruchōrŏs; from ĕurus (*wide*) and *5561*; *spacious*: - broad."[AF5.20]

"The actual Greek word translated as "strait," (strait gate) in Matthew 17:14 is again *stěnŏs.*[AF5.21]

"However; the actual Greek word translated as "narrow ("*narrow* way") here in Matthew 7:14 is not *stěnŏs*, but rather:

> "2346 thlibō; akin to the base of *5147*; to crowd (lit. or fig.): - afflict, narrow, throng, suffer tribulation, trouble."[AF5.22]

> "5147 tribŏs; from tribō (to "rub"; akin to těirō, truō, and the base of 5131, 5134); a rut or worn track: - path"[AF5.23]

"The actual Greek word translated as "destruction" is:

> "684 apōlěia; from a presumed der. of *622*; *ruin* or *loss* (phys., spiritual or eternal): - damnable (-nation), destruction, die, perdition, x perish, pernicious ways, waste."[AF5.24]

> "622 apŏllumi; from 575 and the base of 3639 to *destroy* fully (reflex. to *perish*, or *lose*), lit. or fig.: - destroy, die, lose, mar, perish."[AF5.25]

"And according to Strong, the *only* time the word *apōlĕia* is ever translated as *destruction* in the entire four gospels, (MMLJ), is in this (Matthew 7:13 KJV), passage.[AF5.26]

"In another unrelated chapter of Matthew, (Matthew 26:8 KJV); when the woman pours the expensive ointment or perfume on Jesus' head, the disciples asked: "'*To what purpose is this waste?*'"[AF5.27] The actual word translated in this passage as "waste," is also *apōlĕia*.[AF5.28]

"Likewise in Mark, (Mark 14:4, KJV); when recounting the same story, the word *apōlĕia* is also translated as "waste" in: "'Why was this waste of the ointment made?'"[AF5.29]

"Thus, it seems that "ruin, loss or waste" represents a better definition or translation of the original Greek word *apōlĕia*, than would be *destruction* or *death*.

"However, one problem with this position; is that there is at least an implied comparison between the translation of *apōlĕia* as destruction or death; because at least at this juncture, it seems that Jesus indicated that those who find this other gate will find life, instead of destruction or death. So because of this, it might also seem fair to consider that the appropriate translation of *apōlĕia* would be as destruction or death; based upon this implied comparison of *apōlĕia* with life; with life being the *opposite* of destruction or death.

"But then again, it must be asked that if *destruction* or *death*, instead of *waste*, were the correct meaning for what Jesus spoke in Aramaic; then why was it that the above "*apŏllumi*; "... to *destroy* fully (reflex. to *perish*, or *lose*), lit. or fig.: - destroy, die, lose, mar, perish," was not chosen as the most synonymic Greek word? Instead it was *apōlĕia*; albeit derived from *apŏllumi*; which was chosen as most synonymic.

"Thus a fair translation of Matthew 17:13, based upon the original Greek would be:

> "*Enter* '(ĕisĕrchŏmal)' *ye in at the* '*narrow from obstacles standing close about* (stĕnŏs)' *gate: for* '*spread out flat* (platus)' *is the gate, and* '(*wide*) *and spacious* (ĕuruchōrŏs)' *is*

the "road, (hŏdŏs) *that leadeth to 'waste ruin or loss,* (apōlĕia),' *and many there be which go in thereat"*

"There is no mention of *salvation*, either here in Matthew 17:13, or in the verses preceding it. So if it can be stipulated that Jesus was *not* speaking about *salvation* here Matthew 17:13, it must be asked precisely what it was of which He was in fact speaking?

"There is the one gate or door that is *narrow* because of obstacles. At this juncture, it is unclear as to precisely what it is that is on the other side of this gate or door.

"And there is another gate or door; that is a "spread out flat" gate; as well as a "wide and spacious" road leading to this "other gate."

"But we are told precisely what is that is on the other side of this "other (wide) gate:" *apōlĕia* or "*waste ruin or loss.*"

"And we are also told, that with respect to this "other," or *apōlĕia*, gate or door: "*many there be which go in thereat*."

"At this juncture; it can reasonably be inferred that if: "*many there be which go in thereat*;" with respect to this second, or "other" (the wide), gate or door; then likely "few" *"there be which go in thereat,"* with regard to the narrow door.

"And the *conclusion* is contained in the very next verse, here again is Matthew 7:14 (KJV):

"Because strait is the gate,
and narrow is the way,
which leadeth unto life,
and few there be that find it."

"Here in verse 14, we are told precisely *why* that which is contained in verse 13 is true, as verse 14 begins with the word: "*because*."

"As previously cited, here the original Greek word for "*strait*" in describing this "*gate*" is again *stĕnŏs*; and the original Greek word translated as "gate" is again *pulē* But with regard to the "*way*," the original Greek word for "narrow" here in describing the "*way*" is not *stĕnŏs*, but rather *thlibō*.

"And we are now told what is on the other side of this particular (verse 14) gate, as *this* gate: "*leadeth unto life, and few there be that find it.*"

"Life means *connection*; and death means *disconnection*. There is *physical life* when the soul is connected to the physical body; and *physical death* when disconnected. There is *spiritual life* when the soul is connected to its original source, (God); and *spiritual death* when disconnected.

"But it seems that *all* to whom these words were spoken, were already *physically* alive. So a fair question for Jesus' audience, would be: "Why should I mess with that *stĕnŏs*, and all of those obstacles close by; when I am already 'alive?'" Or perhaps: "But I am already on the other side of this gate."

"An alternative explanation would be that this "*life*," actually means: "spiritual life;" and so then it actually is *salvation*; just like in Luke; that Jesus was speaking of in these passages. But if this is stipulated as so, then Jesus would have simply "jumped into" this discussion completely out of context.

"Thus we are faced with the choice of believing that Jesus was telling physically alive persons to enter this gate in order to attain physical life; or; that Jesus was referring to "spiritual life," just as in Luke; with *no additional knowledge* available to us in these passages. Or that Jesus was referring to "X."

"The actual Greek word translated here as "life" is:

"2222 zōē; from *2198*; *life* (lit. or fig.): - life (-time). Comp. 5590."[AF5.30]

"2198 zaō; a prim. verb; to *live* (lit. or fig.): - life (-time), (a-) live (-ly), quick."[AF5.31]

"5590 psuchē; from *5594*; *breath*, i.e. (by impl.) *spirit*, abstr. or concr. (the *animal* sentient principle only; thus distinguished on the one hand from *4151*, which is the rational and immortal *soul*; and on the other from 2222 which is mere *vitality*, even of plants: these terms thus exactly correspond respectively to the Heb. 5315, 7307 and 2416): - heart (+- ily), life, mind, soul, + us, + you."[AF5.32]

"4151 pněuma; from *4154*; a *current* of air, i.e. *breath* (*blast*) or a *breeze*; by anal. or fig. a *spirit*, i.e. (human) the rational *soul*, (by impl.) *vital principle*, mental *disposition*, etc., or

> (superhuman) an *angel*, *doemon*, or (divine) *God*, Christ's *spirit*, the Holy *Spirit*: - ghost, life, spirit(ual, ually), mind. Comp. 5590."[AF5:33]

"Here in the definition of *psuchē*, as per Strong's suggested comparison of *zōē* with 5590 *psuchē*, distinctions are easily seen. Here it is "mere *vitality*, even of plants," which represents the definition of *zōē*, as appears in the definition of *psuchē*.

"Neither the immaterial part of man as *psuchē*: "the *animal* sentient principle only;" nor the immaterial part of man as *pnĕuma*: "the rational and immortal *soul*;" is not only not included in the definition of *zōē*, but each are specifically *excluded* from being in the definition of *zōē*—at least according to Strong.

"Since it is only *pnĕuma*, and some may even argue *psuchē*; that is or are in need of *salvation*; and since it appears that each is *precluded* from being included in the definition of *zōē*; it could not have been *salvation*, (the *means* for attaining *spiritual* life), about which Jesus was speaking at that time, as per what is contained here in Matthew.

> "And since all that could hear Jesus at that time were already physically alive, it could not have been *physical* life about which, ("*leadeth to*") Jesus was speaking at that time."[8.5]

What Jesus was speaking about here, was the *apōlĕia*, or: "*waste ruin or loss*" of one's: "zōē; from *2198*; *life* (lit. or fig.): - life (-time);" which is derived from "zaō; a prim. verb; to *live* (lit. or fig.)." This is what happens to one's "lifetime," if that "*gate*" which is "*wide*;" to which the "*way*" is "*broad*;" is chosen—the "*gate*" that: "*many there be which go in thereat.*"

This is not the "*waste ruin or loss*" of man's *physical* life. This is not the "*waste ruin or loss*" of man's *spiritual* life; i.e.; loss of salvation. This is the "*waste ruin or loss*" of man's "lifetime." Meaning; the *purpose* for man's lifetime as stated in Genesis 1:28, when man is instructed by God to *kâbash*; (In English: Put the kibosh on.); the earth; and man later being referred to by God as *tsâbâ'*: "a *mass* of persons (or fig. things), espec. reg. organized for war (an *army*)."

And of course this "*wide*" "*waste ruin or loss*" "*gate*" is "*wide*" because there are little or no *stĕnŏs* because of obstacles placed there by the enemy. In addition, the "*way*" to this "gate" is "*broad*" because there is no *thlibō*: "to crowd (lit. or fig.): - afflict, narrow, throng, suffer tribulation, trouble;" deliberately placed there to be "in the way."

These *stĕnŏs*, or "*narrow* (from obstacles *standing* close about);" and these *thlibō*, or: "to crowd (lit. or fig.): - afflict, narrow, throng, suffer tribulation, trouble;" are all reserved for, and dedicated to; the gate where man's *zōē*, or "lifetime," will *not* be subject to: *"waste ruin or loss."*

It is that which *thlibō* or *crowds*, that man must overcome to get to that "lifetime" gate. That which is trying to prevent an individual from getting to this *zōē* gate, fears the results if any man should become one of the *"few there be that find it."*

On the other side of this *"gate"* lie wisdom and power in quantities difficult to even imagine. And once one gets there, they become essentially unstoppable—at least while they are physically alive.

This *zōē "gate"* is custom made for each human being. There is a lock on this "gate" that automatically opens once the person for whom it is custom designed gets to this "gate." The enemy, or those that *thlibō* or *crowds* the *"way;"* must stop the arrival by crowding, or *thlibō* the *"way;"* and/or by placing obstacles, or *stĕnŏs*.

It is the inability to get through the crowding, and or the obstacles; that is the true reason for the "Apostolic Era Only" excuse for lack of *dunamis*.

The first *four* books of the New Testament: Matthew, Mark, Luke, and John, are about *Jesus*; or the *Second* Part of the Trinity. The *fifth* book of the New Testament, the book of "Acts;" is about the *Christ*, or the *Third* Part of the Trinity. It is the power of the Holy Ghost that increases this ability to act—hence the name: "Book of Acts."

As one progressively overcomes the *crowding*, and the *obstacles* to this "*gate*;" there are increasing levels of the Holy Ghost being *on* him and *in* him. Once this "*gate*" is entered, the Holy Ghost is fully *in* Him. This is the "helper" promised by Jesus, who will provide the wisdom and power to perform "*works*" even "*greater*" than those done by Jesus.

And upon entering this "gate," structure and function become one. Meaning; that the unique design of that particular host by God to perform certain functions; and the capabilities to perform those same functions are "in synch."

This means the enemy must go to "Plan C."

"Plan A" was based upon maintaining the *ignorance* of the host. "Plan B" was the *crowding* and the placement of *obstacles*. These two "Plans," are much easier for the enemy; as there is much specificity; and there is always that "*wide*" gate, and that "*broad*" way; as a diversion to get a host to: "take the easy way in."

But once the *zōē*, or "lifetime" gate is reached, everything changes. Now the enemy is forced to fight that which represents essentially incalculable amounts of wisdom and power; and most importantly *unpredictability*.

9

The Gay Circuit

Dunamis or *supernatural* power, is not the same as *gay*; but that which provides this *dunamis* or *supernatural* power simultaneously causes *gay*—if permitted to do so.

It must again be stated what literal *gay* is not. *Gay* is not homosexuality. This usage of *gay* to describe homosexuality is somewhat recent; and is part of a much larger plan. And this is *not* a plan perpetrated *by* homosexuals—except perhaps tangentially. Rather; a better argument exists that it is a plan done *to* homosexuals, and perpetrated by those very same forces that man as *tsâbâ'* is instructed by God to *kâbash*.

It is the removal of man's *reality* of the literal definition of *gay*; by the supplanting of this *reality* with the *reality* of homosexuality that is the objective. Why homosexuality? Because over millennia; those who are or were charged with telling us what God's word said, either knew little of what was they were speaking; or simply lie or lied to us about God's actual views regarding homosexuality—at least according to a reasonable read of the original Hebrew and Greek.

The destruction of Sodom had nothing to do with homosexuality directly. The *only* relationship that can be established between any of the "goings on" at Sodom, and homosexuality; is based upon the non-literal meaning of just one word: *yâda'*; which again literally means: "to *know* (prop. to ascertain by *seeing*)." Thus any relationship to homosexuality requires a mistranslation, by assuming the *euphemistic* use of *yâda'*; when the literal meaning seems much more likely.

Of course these men in the crowd were lying about wanting to: "to *know* (prop. to ascertain by *seeing*)" these men. This was a *ruse* to get them to a place where they could be killed. But their lying about their true intentions; is not the same thing as telling the truth about a different intention.

And it seems that one of the main participants, Lot, did not believe this "non-literal" meaning of *yâda'* was what was meant—else why offer two young *females*, to *male homosexuals*? It is true that Lot utilized this one word euphemistically; and thus non-literally. But with Lot, this word was used in describing a *female-male* event that had never occurred.

So today the destruction of Sodom, (and Gomorrah); is believed by most to not be because of the level of wickedness and evil actually "going on;" but largely because of homosexuality. This belief is and was so widespread, that the word "sodomy" was invented based upon the name of this city—even though as previously seen, Çᵉdôm means: "to *scorch*; *burnt* (i.e. *volcanic* or *bituminous*) district;" and refers only to the nature of the area or "district;" and not in any way either the nature of, or sexual proclivities of, the inhabitants of Sodom.

Thus: "If you want to know how evil homosexuality is, look at what God did to Sodom and Gomorrah;" is at best a display of Biblical ignorance; or at worst, an outright lie. What God did to these cities was because of massive evil and wickedness; and not because of homosexuality in any significant way—at least if His literal written Word is considered a reliable source.

Nevertheless, the common but false *reality* of God's "view" of homosexuality remained. In the eyes of many, homosexuality was the "sinner's sin," or the "unforgivable sin." Some cultures murdered homosexuals, and this continues even today.

This is not to say that homosexuality is not a sin in the Biblical sense, as it clearly is. But this "missing the mark" is likely because of the difficulties homosexuality causes with any meaningful compliance with the: "*Be fruitful, and multiply, and replenish the earth,*" part of the instructions given by God to man in Genesis 1:28.

However, unlike most other sins, homosexuality alone has no victim; i.e.; there is no harm, or *nocere*, done to anyone without their consent—if it is homosexuality alone. This concept of injury to another; forms the basis of man's law, which was originally derived from God's law. Thus homosexuality alone is this sense literally *innocent*, as *innocent* is derived from *non-nocere*, or: "no harm."

Understanding this purported but false level of the "sinfulness" of homosexuality in "God's eye," is important in understanding precisely why the enemy did what he did with the word *gay*; and also *reveals* much.

As one approaches the *zōē* or "lifetime" "*gate*" discussed in the previous chapter; one becomes "gayer and gayer" in the *literal* sense. [This actual *process* will be addressed in greater detail shortly.]

And so the enemy, who greatly fears any individual getting even close to this *zōē* "gate;" i.e.; becoming one of the *"few there be that find it;"* decided to act. He took the word, "gay," which provides the best description of the visible condition of one who is approaching or has entered this *zōē* "gate;" and changed the meaning to that which he had previously convinced many others to lie about. Namely: the level of "sinfulness" of homosexuality.

As stated earlier, this then forces the utilization of other words to describe that which was previously best described as "gay." And since perfect synonyms rarely exist in the same language, the original true meaning of *gay* was at best severely diminished, and at worst, lost.

And since words are symbols used to create *realities* about *actualities*; the precise and/or total *reality* of what literal "gay" actually represents, was likewise lost. The use of the present tense in "represents" here is done purposefully; as changing a *reality*, does nothing to change an *actuality*.

And given the chronic, pernicious, worldwide, (and unjustified) *hatred* for homosexuality and homosexuals; this virtually guarantees that *gay* would cease to be used to describe anything *except* homosexuality. If this is in any way doubted, one merely need research how many newborns are named "Gaylord" today.

There can only be one *worst* sin; the one that is erroneously believed to justify the total and complete destruction of Sodom, and Lot's wife. If this "worst of all possible sins" were considered to be money, it is revealing to see how the enemy spent this money.

Earlier *glad* and *joy* were distinguished. *Gladness* was previously defined as "bright, shining;" and *gay* was similarly defined. But again, there is a difference.

In the case of *gladness*, the "bright, shining" is caused by, and thus is a *reflection* of, that which is *within*, and as stated; is thus limited to that which is within.

But with regard to *gay*, the bright, and shining the is result of that which is *without*; and thus is not limited by that which is within—except for cooperation with that which is without.

Gladness is similar to a *reflector*; but *gay* is similar to a *lamp*. But this should be further analyzed.

The lamp of *gay* is powered by that which is without. Thus in this sense gay is also a reflector.

First, the noun *lampas*, or "*lamp* or *flambeau*;" engages in the action described by the verb *lampō*, or: "to *beam*, i.e. *radiate* brilliancy." We then *phōs*, or: "*shine* or make *manifest*, espec. by *rays... luminousness*;" or: *phōtĕinŏs*; "*lustrous*, i.e. *transparent* or *well illuminated*." But we are not merely now *lampas*, but rather luchnŏs;, or: "a portable *lamp* or other *illuminator* (lit. or fig.)."

As previously stated: "*Dunamis* or *supernatural* power, is not the same as *gay*; but that which provides this *dunamis* or *supernatural* power, simultaneously causes *gay*—if permitted to do so."

It is the power of the Holy Ghost that is responsible for each.

This exposes another trick perpetrated by the enemy. In causing those upon whom many rely upon for Biblical truth, to change the: "Holy Ghost," to the: "Holy Spirit;" the precise *perceived* function, (reality), of the same is likewise changed. A *ghost* is an immaterial entity that is designed to reside in a physical body. But "spirit," which is derived from the Latin *spiritus*, roughly meaning: "breath like;" could refer to a myriad of immaterial entities. These usages could even include: "evil spirit."

So here with this change from Holy Ghost to Holy Spirit; the emphasis on the function of this entity being "*in us;*" as opposed to merely being "*on us;*" is reduced.

The human being is like an electrical circuit. An *inductor*, or coil; will allow direct current to flow, but will oppose alternating current. A *capacitor* will do the reverse.

Likewise, man is both a "conductor" and a "resistor" by design. Man is designed to *conduct* that which is of God; and *resist* that which is not of God. But man has free will; and thus has a choice in that which he *conducts*, and that which he *resists*.

The very purpose of both the Word of God, and the lies of the enemy; is to influence that which man chooses to "conduct;" and influence that which man chooses to "resist." If man is fed the lies of the enemy, while believing that this is the Word of God; then making the correct choice as to what to *conduct*, and what to *resist*, by "informed consent;" becomes difficult or impossible.

And man will begin to resemble that which he chooses to conduct. This is why as one approaches the *zōē*, or "lifetime," "*gate*" discussed in the previous chapter; one becomes "gayer and gayer" in the *literal* sense.

In the case of demonic possession—even in the movies; no one who is demonically possessed is ever portrayed as "bright" or "shining." Instead, they likewise resemble that which is in *them*.

God is the ultimate source of all literal light; as well as a myriad of other meanings. When man decides to allow that which is of God to flow through him, then the results in him become some *subset* of that *set* known as God. It is the "Holy Ghost" part of God that is available to man; and thus the available power is limited only to that which is conducted. But the free will of man must choose to be this conductor, or perhaps better stated: "Decide what the level of resistance is to be."

Earlier, the one and only time the word "gay" appears in the KJV Bible, in James 2:3, was cited: "*And ye have respect to him that weareth the gay clothing...*" And this original word was *lampas*: "a "*lamp*" or *flambeau*: - lamp, light, torch."

And earlier in Ephesians 5:8-9 (KJV) we were told: "*For ye were sometimes darkness, but now are ye light in the Lord: walk as children of light: (For the fruit of the Spirit is in all goodness and righteousness and truth.)*"

Here the *reason* ("*for*," or because), we: "*now are*," "*light in the Lord*;" or *phōs*; "(to *shine* or make *manifest*, espec. by *rays... luminousness*;" is that: "*the fruit of the*" *lampō*, or again: "to *beam*, i.e. *radiate* brilliancy (lit. or fig): - give light, shine;" "*is in all goodness and righteousness and truth*." And this is the same reason given as to why we are: "*children of light*;" or this same *phōs*.

It must be asked if it is *because* of the "*fruit*" of this verb *lampō*, or "to *beam*, i.e. *radiate* brilliancy," (now translated as "*Spirit*," but originally translated as "light"); that: "*is in all goodness and righteousness and truth*;" that we *phōs*: "*shine* or make *manifest*, espec. by *rays... luminousness*;" and we "*walk as children of*," *phōs*?

This *lampō*, or light, or now translated as "*Spirit*," is the *source*. If we lower the resistance of our circuit, and allow this to flow through us, we then *phōs*, or: "*shine* or make *manifest*, espec. by *rays... luminousness*."

Where is this *lampō* to be found? It would seem that seeking: "*goodness and righteousness and truth*," would be a good place to start; as we are told that its "*fruit*," "*is in all*" of these things. But it is the *fruit* of *lampō* that is found here, and not the *lampō* itself.

The *phōs* is like the reflected, or *passive* light of the moon; while the *lampō* is like the actual, or active *light* of the sun. Thus the fruit of that which is *reflected* should also be in: "*goodness and righteousness and truth*." And this does in fact happen when we "*walk as children of*," this *phōs*.

But there is another component to true gay. The same is the offspring of *faith*, but is not the offspring of "blind faith" often associated with religion, or other so called "spiritual matters."

Earlier, the most common word translated as faith in the New Testament was provided. The same was: "4102 pistis; from 3982; *persuasion*, i.e. *credence*;..." and is translated as: "assurance, belief, believe, faith, fidelity." And *pistis* is derived from: "3982 pĕithō; a prim. verb; to *convince* (by argument, true or false)..."

Thus *faith* here in this usage, is the result of *persuasion* from being *convinced*. And the referenced *offspring* of this faith is *confidence*—which is literally derived from the prefix: *con*, or with; and the root: *fidelis* or *faith*. And this *confidence* results in an *attitude* consistent with the same.

Thus one who is *gay*, is visibly "bright and shining" from that which is *without*, and the above passages reasonably explain this mechanism. But there is also that high level of *confidence* that something good will happen—even if there is no knowledge as to precisely what this "good" thing will be. This confidence in some good thing happening part, could be referred to as *joy*; as opposed to either hope or happiness.

Thus it could be said that gay = joy + "bright and shining." This *gay* permeates one's behavior, and remains at some level, no matter what the circumstances.

As previously discussed, *gay* is different than *hope*, as hope is *desire* plus *expectation* for some specific event; with this expectation being with some *level* of *confidence*, (which may be oxymoronic); but this is different than actually being *confident*—here confident meaning: a level of confidence approaching or being at the: "knowing for certain" point.

It cannot be overemphasized, that *gay* and *dunamis* occur together—if it is actual *gay* and not merely *gladness*. Again, *gladness* comes from that which is *within*, and is limited to that which is within; but *gay* comes from that which is *without*, and thus is unlimited, even to the point of the associated level of *dunamis* being able to do greater works than Jesus did—at least according to Jesus.

Gay represents a low resistance circuit to *lampō*, and results in *phōs*. Gay also represents a low resistance circuit to *dunamis*, and results in virtually unlimited levels of supernatural ability.

But just as the case in the "Talent Man" parable about *dunamis*, becoming gay is also a *process*. And the acquisition of *pistis*; is also a process, or series of processes.

These processes occur on the "*way*" to that *zōē*, or "lifetime" gate. The purpose of that which *thlibō*, or *crowds*, this "*way*" to the *zōē*, or "lifetime" gate is to stop these processes. And this "crowding" must be overcome to get to that *zōē*, or "lifetime" gate. It must be remembered that this *thlibō* is on the *path* or the "*way*" to this gate; and not at the gate itself.

Thus for obvious reasons; that which *thlibō*, fear anyone's acquisition of "gay;" as this increased power, and impervious mental state; represent significant threats to them. And what these especially fear, is anyone eventually getting to this *zōē* "gate;" i.e.; become one of the "*few there be that find it.*" On the other side of this "*gate*" lie wisdom and power in quantities difficult to even imagine. And again, once one gets there, they become essentially unstoppable—at least while they are physically alive.

So it would make sense for those that *thlibō* or *crowd* the "*way*," to try and find some way to "erase" the true meaning of *gay*. This is because, as previously discussed, once the word that symbolizes the state of being *gay* is lost; then the *knowledge* of that *gay* state is at a minimum altered, and more likely lost—unless another word is agreed upon. But in order to agree upon another word, one would first need to have some level of knowledge about the actuality. This supplanting is an attempt by the enemy to enhance the aforementioned: "Plan A."

And as some type of "insurance policy," here this "new" meaning for gay; represents that which most, (erroneously), believe to be a sin of such magnitude, that Sodom was completely destroyed because of it.

Interestingly; somewhere around the time Ms. Stein introduced her "writing," (circa 1922); in furtherance of the distribution of the "new meaning" of or for *gay*; a song was written.

> *"This little light of mine, I'm gonna let it shine... let it shine. Won't let Satan blow it out, I'm gonna let it shine...let it shine. Hide it under a bushel , No, I gonna let it shine... let it shine..."*
>
> Harry Dixon Loes
> Public Domain, circa 1922

This was a rather "brilliant" scheme, or schemes by the enemy. Whether or not it ultimately succeeds, depends upon each of us; and thus remains to be determined.

—*Leslie F. Chiffon*

Glossary

a (H): "1 a; of Heb. or.; the first letter of the alphabet; fig. only (from its us as a numeral) the *first*: - alpha. Often used (usually an, before a vowel) also in composition as a contraction from 427) in the sense of *privation*; so in many words beginning with this letter; occasionally in the sense of *union* (as a contraction of *260*)."[3.31]

abussŏs (G): "12 abussŏs; from *1* (as a neg. particle) and a var. of *1037*; *depthless*, i.e. (spec.) (infernal) "*abyss*": - deep, (bottomless) pit."[6.2]

adŏkimŏs (G): "96 adŏkimŏs; from *1* (as a neg. particle) and *1384*; *unapproved* i.e. *rejected*; by impl. *worthless* (lit. or mor.)…"[2.53] "167 akatharsia; from *169*; *impurity* (the quality), phys. or mor.: - uncleanness"[2.38]

aggĕlŏs (G): "32 aggĕlŏs; from aggĕllō; (prob. der. from *71*; comp. *34*) (to *bring tidings*); a *messenger*; esp. an "*angel*"; by impl. a *pastor*:- angel, messenger."[OAI4]

'am ("5971 'am; from 6004 a *people* (as a congregated *unit*); spec. a *tribe* (as those of Israel); hence (collect.) *troops* or *attendants*; fig. a flock: - folk, men, nation, people"[2.15]

antimisthia (G): "489 antimisthia; from a comp. of 473 and *3408*; *requital, correspondence*: - recompense."[2.51]

'âphâr (H): "6083 'âphâr from 6080; dust (as powdered or gray); hence clay, earth, mud: - ashes, dust, earth, ground, morter, powder, rubbish."[5.4]

apōlĕia (G): "684 apōlĕia; from a presumed der. of *622*; *ruin* or *loss* (phys., spiritual or eternal): - damnable (- nation), destruction, die, perdition, x perish, pernicious ways, waste."[AF5.24]

apŏllumi (G): "622 apŏllumi; from 575 and the base of *3639* to *destroy* fully (reflex. to *perish*, or *lose*), lit. or fig.: - destroy, die, lose, mar, perish."[AF5.25]

apŏthnēskō (H): "599 apŏthnēskō; from 575 and *2348*; to *die* off (lit. or fig): - be dead, death, die, lie a-dying, be slain (x with)."[6.13]

arrhēn (G): "730 arrhēn; or arsēn; prob. from *142*; *male* (as stronger for *lifting*): - male, man."[2.63]

arsĕnŏkŏitēs (G): "733 arsĕnŏkŏitēs; from 730 and *2845*; a *sodomite*: - abuser of (that defile) self with mankind."[2.62]

'âsâh (H): "6213 'âsâh; a prim. root; to do or make, in the broadest sense and widest application..."[4.16]

axiŏs (G): "514 axiŏs; prob. from *71*; *deserving*, *comparable* or *suitable* (as if *drawing* praise): - due, reward, meet, [un-] worthy."[2.57]

bârâ' (H): "1254 bârâ', a prim. root; (absol.) to create; (qualified) to cut down (a wood), select, feed (as formative processes): - choose, create (creator), cut down, dispatch, do, make (fat)."[4.3] "The verb expresses creation out of nothing..."[4.4]

chairō (G): "5463 chairō; a prim. verb; to *be "cheer" ful*, i.e. calmly *happy* or well-off; impers. espec. as salutation (on meeting or parting), *be well*: - farewell, be glad, Godspeed, greeting, hail, joy(-fully), rejoice."[7.6]

charis (G): "5485 charis; from 5463; *graciousness* (as *gratifying*), of manner or act (abstr. or concr.; lit., fig. or spiritual; espec. the divine influence upon the heart, and its reflection in the life; including *gratitude*)..."[7.5]

charisma (G): "5486 charisma; from *5483*; a (divine) *gratuity*, i.e. *deliverance* (from danger or passion); (spec.) a (spiritual) *endowment*, i.e. (subj.) religious *qualification* or obj.) miraculous *faculty*: - (free) gift."[7.8]

charizŏmai (G): "5483 charizŏmai; mid. from 5485; to grant as a *favor* i.e. gratuitously, in kindness, pardon or rescue: - deliver, (frankly) forgive, (freely) give, grant."[7.7]

chasma (G): "5490 chasma; from a form of an obsol. prim. chaō (to "gape" or "yawn"); a "chasm" or vacancy (impassable interval): - gulf."[6.8]

châṭâ' (H): "2398 châṭâ'; a prim. root; prop. to *miss*; hence (fig. and gen.) to *sin*; by infer. to *forfeit*, *lack*, *expiate*, *repent*, (causat.) *lead astray*, *condemn*..."[2.11]

chaṭṭâ'âh (H): "2403 chaṭṭâ'âh; or chaṭṭâ'th; from 2398; and *offense* (sometimes habitual *sinfulness*), and its penalty, occasion, sacrifice, or expiation; also (concr.) an *offender*: - punishment (of sin), purifying (-fication for sin), sin (-ner, offering)."[2.10]

chōra (G): "5561 chōra; fem. of a der. of the base of 5490 through the idea of empty expanse; room, i.e. a space of territory (more or less extensive; often includ. its inhab.): - coast, county, fields, ground, land, region."[6.7]

chrēsis (G): "5540 chrēsis; from 5530; *employment*, i.e. (spec.) sexual *intercourse* (as an occupation of the body): - use's."[2.41]

dōrŏn (G): "1435 dōrŏn; a *present*; spec. a *sacrifice*: - gift, offering."[7.9]

dunamis: (G) supernatural power "*1411* dunamis; from *1410*; *force* (lit. or fig.); spec. miraculous *power* (usually by impl. a *miracle* itself)..."[7.17]

dynamikós: (G) natural power, "from Greek *dynamikós* powerful, from *dynamis* power, from *dynasthai* be able, have power;"[7.16]

ĕis (G): "1519 ĕis; a prim. prep.; to or into (indicating the point reached or entered), of place, time, or (fig.) purpose (result, etc.); also in adv. phrases..."[2.49]

'ĕnôwsh (H): "582 'ĕnôwsh; from 605; prop. a *mortal* (and thus differing from the more dignified 120); hence a *man* in gen. (singly or collect.)..."[2.14]

ĕrgŏn (G): 2041 ĕrgŏn; from a prim. (but obsol.) ĕrgō (to *work*); *toil* (as an effort or occupation); by impl. an *act*: - deed, doing, labour, work."[7.13]

ĕuruchōrŏs (G): "2149 ĕuruchōrŏs; from ĕurus (*wide*) and *5561*; *spacious*: - broad."[AF5.20]

ĕxĕrchŏmai (G): "1831 ĕxĕrchŏmai; from *1537* and *2064*; to *issue* (lit. or fig.): - come - (forth, out), depart (out of), escape, get out..."[6.11]

gay: "*adj.* Probably about 1300, splendid or beautiful; earlier, as a surname (1178); borrowed from Old French *gai* gay, merry; perhaps from Frankish (compare Old High German *gāhi* rapid, impetuous, modern German *jäh* hasty, sudden).

The meaning of joyous or merry appeared probably about 1380. The slang sense of homosexual is first recorded in 1951, apparently shortened from an earlier compound gay cat homosexual boy (about 1935, in underworld and prison slang), but used earlier for a young tramp or hobo, often one attached to an older tramp and usually with a connotation of homosexuality (1897, in American English slang). —n. a homosexual. 1971, American English..."[3.5]

glad: "1909 ĕpi; a prim. prep. prop. mean. *superimposition* (of time, place, order, etc.), as a relation of *distribution* [with the gen.], i.e. *over, upon*, etc.; of *rest* (with the dat.] *at, on*, etc.; of *direction* (with the acc.) *towards, upon*, etc...."[2.48]
"*adj*. Probably before 1200 *glad* joyful, merry, mild, gracious, pleased, in Layamon's *Chronicle of Britian*; developed from Old Engish *glæd* bright, shining, joyous, glad (about 725, in *Beowulf*); cognate with Old Frisian *gled* smooth, Old Saxon *glad*- (in compounds such as *gladmōdi* joyous, happy)..."[3.4]

hamartano (G): "264 hamartano, perh. from 1 (as a neg. particle) and the base of 3313; prop. to miss the mark (and so not share in the prize), i.e. (fig.) to err, esp. (mor.) to sin; - for your faults, offend, sin, trespass."[2.70]

hamartia (G): "266 hamartia; from 264; sin (prop. abstr.): - offence, sin (-ful)."[2.69]

haplŏus (G): "573 haplŏus; prob. from *1* (as a particle of union) and the base of *4120*; prop. *folded together*, i.e. *single* (fig. clear): - single."[3.29]

hell: "Old English hel, helle, "nether world, abode of the dead, infernal regions, place of torment for the wicked after death," from Proto-Germanic *haljō "the underworld" (source also of Old Frisian helle, Old Saxon hellia, Dutch hel, Old Norse hel, German Hölle, Gothic halja "hell"). "Literally "concealed place" (compare Old Norse hellir "cave, cavern"), from PIE root *kel-(1) "to cover, conceal, save." The English word may be in part from Old Norse mythological Hel (from Proto-Germanic *halija "one who covers up or hides something"), in Norse mythology the name of Loki's daughter who rules over the evil dead in Niflheim, the lowest of all worlds (nifl "mist"). A pagan concept and word fitted to a Christian idiom. "In Middle English, also of the Limbus Patrum, place where the Patriarchs, Prophets, etc. awaited the Atonement."[OAI12]

hōs (G): "5613 hōs; prob. adv. of comp. from *3739*; *which how*, i.e. *in that manner* (very variously used, as follows)..."[3.26]

infernal: "*adj.* about 1385 *infernal* of hell, in Chaucer's *Canterbury Tales*; borrowed from Old French *infernal*, from Late Latin *īnfernālis* belonging to the lower regions, from *īnfernus* hell, literally, the lower world, noun use of Latin *īnfernus* situated below, of the lower regions, lower, related to *īnfernus* below; see UNDER."[OAI13]

isaggĕlŏs (G) "2465 siaggĕlŏs; from *2470* and *32*; *like an angel*, i.e. *angelic*: - equal unto the angels."[OAI5]

kâbad (H): "3513 kâbad; or kâbêd; a prim. root; to *be heavy*, i.e. in a bad sense (*burdensome, severe, dull*) or in a good sense numerous, *rich, honorable*); causat. to *make weighty* (in the same two senses)..."[2.12]

kâbash (H): "3533 kâbash; a prim. root; to *tread* down; hence neg. to *disregard*; pos. to *conquer, subjugate, violate*: - bring into bondage, force, keep under, subdue, bring into subjection."[4.12]

kâlâh (H): "3615 kâlâh; a prim. root; to *end*, whether intrans. (to *cease, be finished, perish*) or trans. (to *complete, prepare, consume*)..."[4.14]

kata (G): "2596 kata; a prim. particle; (prep.) *down* (in place or time), in varied relations (according to the case [gen., dat. or acc.] with which it is joined)..."[2.46]

kathēkō (G): "2520 kathēkō; from 2596 and 2240; to reach to, i.e. (neut. of pres. act. part., fig. as adj.) becoming: - convenient fit."[2.55]

kŏitē (G): "2845 kŏitē; from *2749*; a *couch*; by extens. *cohabitation*; by impl. the male *sperm*: - bed, chambering, x conceive."[2.64]

lampas (G): "2985 lampas; from *2989*; a "*lamp*" or *flambeau*: - lamp, light, torch"[3.8]

lampō (G): "2989 lampō a prim. verb; to *beam*, i.e. *radiate* brilliancy (lit. or fig): - give light, shine."[3.9]

limbo: "Latin (in) *limbō* (on) the edge, ablative case of *limbus* edge, border..."[OAI11]

lŏgŏs (G): "*3056* lŏgŏs; from *3004*; something *said* (including the *thought*); by impl. a *topic* (subject of discourse), also *reasoning* (the mental faculty) or *motive*; by extens. a *computation*; spec. (with the art. In John) the Divine *Expression* (i.e. *Christ*)..."[WENJAT29]

luchnŏs (G): "3088 luchnŏs; from the base of *3022*; a portable *lamp* or other *illuminator* (lit. or fig.): - candle, light."[3.32]

machaira (G): "*3162* machaira; prob. fem. of a presumed der. of *3163*; a *knife*, i.e. *dirk*; fig. *war*, judicial *punishment*: - sword."[WENJAT25]

mal'âk (H): "4397 mal'âk; from an unused root mean. to *dispatch* as a deputy; a *messenger*; spec. of God, i.e. an *angel* (also a prophet, priest or teacher): - ambassador, angel, king, messenger"[2.6]

malakŏs (G): "3120 malakŏs; of uncert. affin.; *soft*, i.e. *fine* (clothing); fig. a *catamite*: - effeminate, soft."[2.60]

mammōnas (G): "3126 mammōnas; of Chald. or. (*confidence*, i.e. fig. *wealth*, personified); *mammonas*, i.e. *avarice* (deified): - mammon."[3.38]

massâ' (H): "4853 massâ' from 5375; a burden; spec. tribute, or (abstr.) porterage; fig. an utterance, chiefly a doom, espec. singing; mental desire: - burden, carry away, prophesy..."[7.18]

mĕizōn (G): "3187 mĕizōn; irreg. compar. of 3173; *larger* (lit. or fig., spec. in age): - elder, greater (-est), more."[7.14]

m*ᵉ'*ôd (H): "3966 mᵉ'ôd; from the same as 181; prop. *vehemence*, i.e. (with or without prep.) *vehemently*; by impl. *wholly*, *speedily*, etc. (often with other words as an intensive or superlative; espec. when repeated)..."[2.13]

mĕtallassō (G): "3337 mĕtallassō; from *3326* and *236*; to *exchange*: - change."[2.39]

nether: "1: situated down or below: lower; 2: situated or believed to be situated beneath the earth's surface."[OAI10]

nŏus (G): "3563 nŏus; prob. from the base of *1097*; the *intellect*, i.e. *mind* (divine or human; in thought, feeling or will); by impl. *meaning*: - mind, understanding. Comp. 5590"[2.54]

para (G): "3844 para; a prim. prep.; prop. *near*, i.e. (with gen.) *from*, *beside* (lit. or fig.), (with dat.) *at* (or *in*) the *vicinity* of (obj. or subj.), (with acc.) to the *proximity* with (local [espec. *beyond* or *opposed* to] or causal [*on account* of])..."[2.42]

paradidōmi (G) "3860 paradidōmi; from *3844* and *1325*; to *surrender*, i.e. *yield up*, *intrust*, *transmit*..."[2.37]

pĕithō (G): "3982 pĕithō; a prim. verb; to *convince* (by argument, true or false); by anal. to *pacify* or *conciliate* (by other fair means); reflex. or pass. to *assent* (to evidence or authority), to *rely* (by inward certainty): - agree, assure, believe, have confidence, be (wax) [(? unreadable)], make friend, obey, persuade, trust, yield."[3.3]

pĕripatĕō (G): 4043 pĕripatĕō; from *4012* and *3961*; to *tread* all *around*, i.e. *walk* at large (espec. as proof of ability); fig. to *live deport oneself*, *follow* (as a companion or votary): - go, be occupied with, walk (about)."[3.20]

phainō (G): "5316 phainō; prol. for the base of *5457*; to *lighten* (*shine*), i.e. *show* (trans. or intrans., lit. or fig.)..."[3.17]

phēmi (G): "5346 phēmi; prop. the same as the base of *5457* and *5316*; to *show* or *make known* one's thoughts, i.e. *speak* or *say*..."[3.18]

phĕrō (G): "5342 phĕrō; a prim. verb... to "*bear*" or *carry*."[7.20]

phōs (G): "5457 phōs; from an obsol. phaō (to *shine* or make *manifest*, espec. by *rays*; comp. *5316*, *5346*); *luminousness* (in the widest application, nat. or artificial, abstr. or concr., lit. or fig.): - fire, light."[3.16]

phōtĕinŏs (G): "5460 phōtĕinŏs; from 5457; *lustrous*, i.e. *transparent* or *well illuminated* (fig.): - bright, full of light..."[3.28]

phrĕar (G): "5421 phrĕar; of uncert. der.; a *hole* in the ground (dug for obtaining or holding water or other purposes), i.e. a *cistern* or *well*; fig. an *abyss* (as a *prison*): - well, pit."[6.5]

phusikŏs (G): "5446 phusikŏs; from 5449; "*physical*", i.e. (by impl.) *instinctive*: - natural."[2.40]

pistis (G): "4102 pistis; from 3982; *persuasion*, i.e. *credence*; mor. *conviction* (of *religious* truth, or the truthfulness of God or a religious teacher), espec. *reliance* upon Christ for salvation; abstr. *constancy* in such profession; by extens. the system of religious (Gospel) *truth* itself: - assurance, belief, believe, faith, fidelity."[3.2]

planaō (G): "4105 planaō; from *4106*; to (prop. *cause to*) *roam* (from safety, truth, or virtue): - go astray, deceive, err, seduce, wander, be out of the way."[OAI7]

planē (G): "4106 planē; fem. of *4108* (as abstr.); obj. *fraudulence*; subj. a *straying* from orthodoxy or piety..."[2.52]

platus (G): "4116 platus; from *4111*; spread out "*flat*" ("plot"), i.e. *broad*: - wide."[AF5.19]

plĕkō (G): "4120 plĕkō; a prim. word; to *twine* or *braid*: - plait."[3.30]

pnĕuma (G): "*4151* pnĕuma; from *4154*; a *current* of air, i.e. *breath* (*blast*) or a *breeze*; by anal. or fig. a *spirit*, i.e. (human) the rational *soul*, (by impl.) *vital principle*, mental *disposition* etc..."[WENJAT26]

pŏnērŏs (G): "4190 pŏnērŏs; from a der. of *4192*; *hurtful*, i.e. *evil* prop. in effect or influence..."[3.33]

pŏtĕ (G): "4218 pŏtĕ; from the base of *4225* and *5037*; indef. adv., at *some time, ever*: - afore- (any, some-) time (s), at length (the last), (+ n-) ever, in the old time, in time past, once, when."[3.15]

pulē (G): 4439 pulē; appar. a prim. word; a *gate*, i.e. the leaf or wing of a folding *entrance* (lit. or fig.): - gate."[AF5.18]

psuchē (G): "5590 psuchē; from *5594*; *breath*, i.e. (by impl.) *spirit*, abstr. or concr. (the *animal* sentient principle only; thus distinguished on the one hand from *4151*, which is the rational and immortal *soul*; and on the other from *2222* which is mere *vitality*, even of plants: these terms thus exactly correspond respectively to the Heb. 5315, 7307 and 2416): - heart (+- ily), life, mind, soul, + us, + you."[AF5.32]

râ'a (H): "7489 râ'a'; a prim. root; prop. to *spoil* (lit. by *breaking* to pieces); fig. to *make* (or be) *good for nothing*, i.e. *bad* (phys., soc. or mor.)..."[2.21]

râdâh (H) "7287 râdâh; a prim. root; to *tread* down, i.e. *subjugate*; spec. to *crumble* off: - (come to, make to) have dominion, prevail against..."[4.9]

rê'shîyth (H): "7225 rê'shîyth; from the same as 7218; the first, in place, time, order or rank (spec. a firstfruit)...."[4.2]

rhēma (G): "*4487* rhēma; from *4483*; an *utterance* (individ., collect. or spec.); by impl. a *matter* or *topic* (espec. of narration, command or dispute); with a neg. *naught* whatever..."[WENJAT27]

skŏtĕinŏs (G): "4652 skŏtĕinŏs; from *4655 opaque*, i.e. (fig.) *benighted*: - dark, full of darkness."[3.34]

skŏtŏs (G): "4655 skŏtŏs; from the base of *4639*; *shadiness*, i.e. *obscurity* (lit. or fig.): - darkness."[3.19]

Sodom (**Çedôm** H): "5467 Çedôm; from an unused root mean. to *scorch*; *burnt* (i.e. *volcanic* or *bituminous*) district; *Sedom*, a place near the Dead Sea: - Sodom."[2.5]

sōzō (G): "4982 sōzō; from a prim. sōs (contr. for obsol. saŏs "*safe*"); to *save*, i.e. *deliver* or *protect* (lit. or fig.): - heal, preserve, save (self), do well, be (make) whole."[AF5.12]

stĕnŏs (G): "4728 stĕnŏs; prob, from the base of *2476*; *narrow* (from obstacles *standing* close about): - strait."

talantŏn (G): "5007 talantŏn; neut. of a presumed der. of the orig. form of tiaō (to *bear*; equiv. to 5342); a *balance* (as *supporting* weights), i.e. (by impl.) a certain *weight* (and thence a *coin* or rather *sum* of money) or "*talent*": - talent."[7.19]

tĕknŏn (G): "5043 tĕknŏn; from the base of *5088*; a *child* (as *produced*): - child, daughter, son."[3.22]

thanatŏs (G): "2288 thanatŏs; from *2348*; (prop. an adj. used as a noun) *death* (lit. or fig.) : - x deadly, (be . . .) death."[2.58]

thlibō (G): "2346 thlibō; akin to the base of *5147*; to crowd (lit. or fig.): - afflict, narrow, throng, suffer tribulation, trouble."[AF5.22]

την (G): which appears to simply mean "the."[2.50]

tôwʻêbâh (H): "8441 tôwʻêbâh; or tôʻêbâh; fem. act. part. of 8581 prop. something *disgusting* (mor.), i.e. (as noun) an *abhorrence*; espec. *idolatry* or (concr.) an *idol*"[2.32]

tôwl^{e}dâh (H): "8435 tôwl^{e}dâh; or tôl^{e}dâh; from 3205; (plur. only) *descent*, i.e. *family*; (fig.) *history*: - birth, generations."[4.19]

tribŏs (G): "5147 tribŏs; from tribō (to "rub"; akin to tĕirō, truō, and the base of 5131, 5134); a rut or worn track: - path"[AF5.23]

tsâbâ' (H): "6635 tsâbâ' or ts^{e}bâ'âh from 6633; a *mass* of persons (or fig. things), espec. reg. organized for war (an *army*); by impl. a *campaign*, lit. or fig. (spec. *hardship, worship*): -appointed time, (+) army, (+) battle, company, host, service, soldiers, waiting upon, war (fare)."[4.21]

votary: "*n.* person devoted to something, devotee. 1546, person bound by vows to a religious life; formed in English from Latin *vōtum* VOW + English *-ary*..."[3.21]

yâda (H): "3045 yâda'; a prim. root; to *know* (prop. to ascertain by *seeing*); used in a great variety of senses, fig. lit. euphem. and infer. (including *observation, care, recognition*; and causat. *instruction, designation, punishment*, etc.)..."[2.16]

yâtsar (H): "3335 yâtsar; prob. identical with 3334 (through the *squeezing* into shape); ([comp. 3331]); to *mould* into a form; espec. as a *potter*;..."[5.3]

yôwm (H): "3117 yôwm; from an unused root mean. to *be hot*; a *day* (as the *warm* hours), whether lit. (from sunrise to sunset, or from one sunset to the next), or fig. (a space of time defined by an associated term), [often used adv.]..."[4.18]

zaō (G): "2198 zaō; a prim. verb; to *live* (lit. or fig.): - life (-time), (a-) live (-ly), quick."[AF5.31]

zōē (G): "2222 zōē; from *2198*; *life* (lit. or fig.): - life (-time). Comp. 5590."[AF5.30]

Bibliography

1.1 Walker/Quadrakoff. *Alleged Fantasy Volume I - Foundations.* ©2020 Quadrakoff Publications Group, LLC Wilmington DE pp.10-11

1.2 https://www.dca.org.uk/assets/general/Session_3_(13th_August)_Miss_Furr_and_Miss_Skeene_by_Gertrude_Stein. (retrieved 8/10/20)

2.1 Strong, James. *Strong's Exhaustive Concordance of the Bible.* ©1890 James Strong, Madison, NJ p.490

2.2 *King James Bible*, Ephesians 2:8-9

2.3 *Amplified Bible* ©1965 Zondorvan Corp. and The Lockman Foundation, La Habra CA Genesis 19:5

2.4 *New International Version The Holy Bible* ©1973 International Bible Society Genesis 19:5

2.5 Strong, James. *Strong's Exhaustive Concordance of the Bible.* ©1890 James Strong, Madison, NJ p. 82 (Hebrew)

2.6 Strong, James. *Strong's Exhaustive Concordance of the Bible.* ©1890 James Strong, Madison, NJ p. 66 (Hebrew)

2.7 *King James Bible*, Genesis 18:16

2.8 *King James Bible*, Genesis 18:22

2.9 *King James Bible*, Genesis 18:20

2.10 Strong, James. *Strong's Exhaustive Concordance of the Bible*. ©1890 James Strong, Madison, NJ p. 38 (Hebrew)

2.11 Strong, James. *Strong's Exhaustive Concordance of the Bible*. ©1890 James Strong, Madison, NJ p. 38 (Hebrew)

2.12 Strong, James. *Strong's Exhaustive Concordance of the Bible*. ©1890 James Strong, Madison, NJ p. 54 (Hebrew)

2.13 Strong, James. *Strong's Exhaustive Concordance of the Bible*. ©1890 James Strong, Madison, NJ p. 60 (Hebrew)

2.14 Strong, James. *Strong's Exhaustive Concordance of the Bible*. ©1890 James Strong, Madison, NJ p. 14 (Hebrew)

2.15 Strong, James. *Strong's Exhaustive Concordance of the Bible*. ©1890 James Strong, Madison, NJ p. 89 (Hebrew)

2.16 Strong, James. *Strong's Exhaustive Concordance of the Bible*. ©1890 James Strong, Madison, NJ p. 47 (Hebrew)

2.17 *King James Bible*, Genesis 19:6-8

2.18 Strong, James. *Strong's Exhaustive Concordance of the Bible*. ©1890 James Strong, Madison, NJ p. 577

2.19 *King James Bible*, Genesis 19:9-11

2.20 *Interlinear Bible Hebrew Greek English, 1 Volume edition*. © 1976, 1977, 1978, 1979, 1980, 1981, 1984. Second Edition, © 1986 Jay P. Green, Sr., Hendrickson Publishers (Genesis 19:9) p. 15

2.21 Strong, James. *Strong's Exhaustive Concordance of the Bible*. ©1890 James Strong, Madison, NJ p. 110 (Hebrew)

2.22 *King James Bible*, Genesis 18:32

2.23 Strong, James. *Strong's Exhaustive Concordance of the Bible*. ©1890 James Strong, Madison, NJ p. 413

2.24 Strong, James. *Strong's Exhaustive Concordance of the Bible*. ©1890 James Strong, Madison, NJ p. 413

2.25 Strong, James. *Strong's Exhaustive Concordance of the Bible*. ©1890 James Strong, Madison, NJ p. 413

2.26 Strong, James. *Strong's Exhaustive Concordance of the Bible*. ©1890 James Strong, Madison, NJ p. 413

2.27 *King James Bible*, Jeremiah 50:40
2.28 *King James Bible*, Deuteronomy 29:23
2.29 *King James Bible*, Genesis 19:25
2.30 *King James Bible*, Leviticus 18:22
2.31 *King James Bible*, Leviticus 20:13
2.32 Strong, James. *Strong's Exhaustive Concordance of the Bible.* ©1890 James Strong, Madison, NJ p. 123 (Hebrew)
2.33 *King James Bible*, Mark 10:6-9
2.34 *King James Bible*, Mark 10:2-5
2.35 *King James Bible*, Romans 1:26-28
2.36 *King James Bible*, Romans 1:21-25
2.37 Strong, James. *Strong's Exhaustive Concordance of the Bible.* ©1890 James Strong, Madison, NJ p. 54 (Greek)
2.38 Strong, James. *Strong's Exhaustive Concordance of the Bible.* ©1890 James Strong, Madison, NJ p. 9 (Greek)
2.39 Strong, James. *Strong's Exhaustive Concordance of the Bible.* ©1890 James Strong, Madison, NJ p. 47 (Greek)
2.40 Strong, James. *Strong's Exhaustive Concordance of the Bible.* ©1890 James Strong, Madison, NJ p. 77 (Greek)
2.41 Strong, James. *Strong's Exhaustive Concordance of the Bible.* ©1890 James Strong, Madison, NJ p. 78 (Greek)
2.42 Strong, James. *Strong's Exhaustive Concordance of the Bible.* ©1890 James Strong, Madison, NJ p. 54 (Greek)
2.43 Strong, James. *Strong's Exhaustive Concordance of the Bible.* ©1890 James Strong, Madison, NJ p. 30
2.44 Strong, James. *Strong's Exhaustive Concordance of the Bible.* ©1890 James Strong, Madison, NJ p. 30
2.45 Strong, James. *Strong's Exhaustive Concordance of the Bible.* ©1890 James Strong, Madison, NJ p. 30
2.46 Strong, James. *Strong's Exhaustive Concordance of the Bible.* ©1890 James Strong, Madison, NJ p. 39 (Greek)
2.47 Strong, James. *Strong's Exhaustive Concordance of the Bible.* ©1890 James Strong, Madison, NJ p. 30

2.48 Strong, James. *Strong's Exhaustive Concordance of the Bible.* ©1890 James Strong, Madison, NJ p. 30 (Greek)
2.49 Strong, James. *Strong's Exhaustive Concordance of the Bible.* ©1890 James Strong, Madison, NJ p. 26 (Greek)
2.50 Strong, James. *Strong's Exhaustive Concordance of the Bible.* ©1890 James Strong, Madison, NJ p. 1308
2.51 Strong, James. *Strong's Exhaustive Concordance of the Bible.* ©1890 James Strong, Madison, NJ p. 13 (Greek)
2.52 Strong, James. *Strong's Exhaustive Concordance of the Bible.* ©1890 James Strong, Madison, NJ p. 58 (Greek)
2.53 Strong, James. *Strong's Exhaustive Concordance of the Bible.* ©1890 James Strong, Madison, NJ p. 8 (Greek)
2.54 Strong, James. *Strong's Exhaustive Concordance of the Bible.* ©1890 James Strong, Madison, NJ p. 50 (Greek)
2.55 Strong, James. *Strong's Exhaustive Concordance of the Bible.* ©1890 James Strong, Madison, NJ p. 38 (Greek)
2.56 *King James Bible*, Romans 1:29-32
2.57 Strong, James. *Strong's Exhaustive Concordance of the Bible.* ©1890 James Strong, Madison, NJ p. 13 (Greek)
2.58 Strong, James. *Strong's Exhaustive Concordance of the Bible.* ©1890 James Strong, Madison, NJ p. 35 (Greek)
2.59 *King James Bible*, 1 Corinthians 6:9-11
2.60 Strong, James. *Strong's Exhaustive Concordance of the Bible.* ©1890 James Strong, Madison, NJ p. 46 (Greek)
2.61 Strong, James. *Strong's Exhaustive Concordance of the Bible.* ©1890 James Strong, Madison, NJ p. 297
2.62 Strong, James. *Strong's Exhaustive Concordance of the Bible.* ©1890 James Strong, Madison, NJ p. 16 (Greek)
2.63 Strong, James. *Strong's Exhaustive Concordance of the Bible.* ©1890 James Strong, Madison, NJ p. 16 (Greek)
2.64 Strong, James. *Strong's Exhaustive Concordance of the Bible.* ©1890 James Strong, Madison, NJ p. 42 (Greek)
2.65 *King James Bible*, 1 Timothy 1:10-11

2.66 *King James Bible*, 1 Timothy 1:8-9

2.67 Strong, James. *Strong's Exhaustive Concordance of the Bible.* ©1890 James Strong, Madison, NJ p. 251

2.68 Strong, James. *Strong's Exhaustive Concordance of the Bible.* ©1890 James Strong, Madison, NJ p. 930

2.69 Strong, James. *Strong's Exhaustive Concordance of the Bible.* ©1890 James Strong, Madison, NJ p. 10 (Greek)

2.70 Strong, James. *Strong's Exhaustive Concordance of the Bible.* ©1890 James Strong, Madison, NJ p. 10 (Greek)

3.1 Strong, James. *Strong's Exhaustive Concordance of the Bible.* ©1890 James Strong, Madison, NJ p. 330

3.2 Strong, James. *Strong's Exhaustive Concordance of the Bible.* ©1890 James Strong, Madison, NJ p. 58 (Greek)

3.3 Strong, James. *Strong's Exhaustive Concordance of the Bible.* ©1890 James Strong, Madison, NJ p. 57 (Greek)

3.4 *Chambers Dictionary of Etymology*, Copyright ©1988 The H. W. Wilson Company, New York, NY p. 434

3.5 *Chambers Dictionary of Etymology*, Copyright ©1988 The H. W. Wilson Company, New York, NY p. 425

3.6 *Chambers Dictionary of Etymology*, Copyright ©1988 The H. W. Wilson Company, New York, NY p. 1048

3.7 Strong, James. *Strong's Exhaustive Concordance of the Bible.* ©1890 James Strong, Madison, NJ p. 381

3.8 Strong, James. *Strong's Exhaustive Concordance of the Bible.* ©1890 James Strong, Madison, NJ p. 44 (Greek)

3.9 Strong, James. *Strong's Exhaustive Concordance of the Bible.* ©1890 James Strong, Madison, NJ p. 44 (Greek)

3.10 *King James Bible*, James 2:3

3.11 Strong, James. *Strong's Exhaustive Concordance of the Bible.* ©1890 James Strong, Madison, NJ p. 381

3.12 *King James Bible*, Ephesians 5: 8-9

3.13 Strong, James. *Strong's Exhaustive Concordance of the Bible.* ©1890 James Strong, Madison, NJ p. 969

3.14 Strong, James. *Strong's Exhaustive Concordance of the Bible.* ©1890 James Strong, Madison, NJ p. 604

3.15 Strong, James. *Strong's Exhaustive Concordance of the Bible.* ©1890 James Strong, Madison, NJ p. 59 (Greek)

3.16 Strong, James. *Strong's Exhaustive Concordance of the Bible.* ©1890 James Strong, Madison, NJ p. 77 (Greek)

3.17 Strong, James. *Strong's Exhaustive Concordance of the Bible.* ©1890 James Strong, Madison, NJ p. 75 (Greek)

3.18 Strong, James. *Strong's Exhaustive Concordance of the Bible.* ©1890 James Strong, Madison, NJ p. 75 (Greek)

3.19 Strong, James. *Strong's Exhaustive Concordance of the Bible.* ©1890 James Strong, Madison, NJ p. 65 (Greek)

3.20 Strong, James. *Strong's Exhaustive Concordance of the Bible.* ©1890 James Strong, Madison, NJ p. 57 (Greek)

3.21 *Chambers Dictionary of Etymology*, Copyright ©1988 The H. W. Wilson Company, New York, NY p. 1212

3.22 Strong, James. *Strong's Exhaustive Concordance of the Bible.* ©1890 James Strong, Madison, NJ p. 71 (Greek)

3.23 *King James Bible*, Matthew 17:1-3

3.24 Strong, James. *Strong's Exhaustive Concordance of the Bible.* ©1890 James Strong, Madison, NJ p. 919

3.25 Strong, James. *Strong's Exhaustive Concordance of the Bible.* ©1890 James Strong, Madison, NJ p. 603

3.26 Strong, James. *Strong's Exhaustive Concordance of the Bible.* ©1890 James Strong, Madison, NJ p. 79 (Greek)

3.27 *King James Bible*, Matthew 6:22-23

3.28 Strong, James. *Strong's Exhaustive Concordance of the Bible.* ©1890 James Strong, Madison, NJ p. 77 (Greek)

3.29 Strong, James. *Strong's Exhaustive Concordance of the Bible.* ©1890 James Strong, Madison, NJ p. 14 (Greek)

3.30 Strong, James. *Strong's Exhaustive Concordance of the Bible.* ©1890 James Strong, Madison, NJ p. 58 (Greek)
3.31 Strong, James. *Strong's Exhaustive Concordance of the Bible.* ©1890 James Strong, Madison, NJ p. 7 (Greek)
3.32 Strong, James. *Strong's Exhaustive Concordance of the Bible.* ©1890 James Strong, Madison, NJ p. 45 (Greek)
3.33 Strong, James. *Strong's Exhaustive Concordance of the Bible.* ©1890 James Strong, Madison, NJ p. 58 (Greek)
3.34 Strong, James. *Strong's Exhaustive Concordance of the Bible.* ©1890 James Strong, Madison, NJ p. 65 (Greek)
3.35 Strong, James. *Strong's Exhaustive Concordance of the Bible.* ©1890 James Strong, Madison, NJ p. 603
3.36 Strong, James. *Strong's Exhaustive Concordance of the Bible.* ©1890 James Strong, Madison, NJ p. 65 (Greek)
3.37 *King James Bible*, Matthew 6:24
3.38 Strong, James. *Strong's Exhaustive Concordance of the Bible.* ©1890 James Strong, Madison, NJ p. 46 (Greek)

4.1 *King James Bible*, Genesis 1:1
4.2 Strong, James. *Strong's Exhaustive Concordance of the Bible.* ©1890 James Strong, Madison, NJ p. 106 (Hebrew)
4.3 Strong, James. *Strong's Exhaustive Concordance of the Bible.* ©1890 James Strong, Madison, NJ p. 23 (Hebrew)
4.4 *Holy Bible Saint Joseph New Catholic Edition*. ©1962, ©1957-1949 Catholic Book Publishing Co., NY. p.15
4.5 *King James Bible*, Genesis 1:2
4.6 *Interlinear Bible Hebrew Greek English, 1 Volume edition*. © 1976, 1977, 1978, 1979, 1980, 1981, 1984. Second Edition, © 1986 Jay P. Green, Sr., Hendrickson Publishers (Genesis 1:2) p. 1
4.7 *King James Bible*, Genesis 1:26
4.8 *King James Bible*, Genesis 1:27

4.9 Strong, James. *Strong's Exhaustive Concordance of the Bible.* ©1890 James Strong, Madison, NJ p. 107 (Hebrew)
4.10 Strong, James. *Strong's Exhaustive Concordance of the Bible.* ©1890 James Strong, Madison, NJ p. 225
4.11 *King James Bible*, Genesis 1:28
4.12 Strong, James. *Strong's Exhaustive Concordance of the Bible.* ©1890 James Strong, Madison, NJ p. 54 (Hebrew)
4.13 *King James Bible*, Genesis 2:1
4.14 Strong, James. *Strong's Exhaustive Concordance of the Bible.* ©1890 James Strong, Madison, NJ p. 55 (Hebrew)
4.15 *King James Bible*, Genesis 2:2-4
4.16 Strong, James. *Strong's Exhaustive Concordance of the Bible.* ©1890 James Strong, Madison, NJ p. 92 (Hebrew)
4.17 Strong, James. *Strong's Exhaustive Concordance of the Bible.* ©1890 James Strong, Madison, NJ p. 225
4.18 Strong, James. *Strong's Exhaustive Concordance of the Bible.* ©1890 James Strong, Madison, NJ p. 48 (Hebrew)
4.19 Strong, James. *Strong's Exhaustive Concordance of the Bible.* ©1890 James Strong, Madison, NJ p. 225
4.20 Strong, James. *Strong's Exhaustive Concordance of the Bible.* ©1890 James Strong, Madison, NJ p. 640
4.21 Strong, James. *Strong's Exhaustive Concordance of the Bible.* ©1890 James Strong, Madison, NJ p. 119 (Hebrew)
4.22 *King James Bible*, Genesis 1:21
4.23 Strong, James. *Strong's Exhaustive Concordance of the Bible.* ©1890 James Strong, Madison, NJ p. 98 (Hebrew)
4.24 *King James Bible*, Numbers 2:3-4
4.25 Strong, James. *Strong's Exhaustive Concordance of the Bible.* ©1890 James Strong, Madison, NJ p. 492
4.26 *King James Bible*, 2 Samuel 10:6-7
4.27 Strong, James. *Strong's Exhaustive Concordance of the Bible.* ©1890 James Strong, Madison, NJ p. 493

5.1 Camminatore, Danté. *Ostium Ab Inferno—The Opening From Hell.* ©2020 Quadrakoff Publications Group, LLC Wilmington DE pp. 8-15

5.2 *King James Bible*, Genesis 2:7

5.3 Strong, James. *Strong's Exhaustive Concordance of the Bible.* ©1890 James Strong, Madison, NJ p. 51 (Hebrew)

5.4 Strong, James. *Strong's Exhaustive Concordance of the Bible.* ©1890 James Strong, Madison, NJ p. 90 (Hebrew)

5.5 *King James Bible*, Genesis 2:8

5.6 *King James Bible*, 1 Corinthians 15:45

5.7 Walker J Bartholomew. *Statists Saving One* ©2017 Quadrakoff Publications Group, LLC Wilmington DE pp. 58-59

6.1 *King James Bible*, Luke 8:31

6.2 Strong, James. *Strong's Exhaustive Concordance of the Bible.* ©1890 James Strong, Madison, NJ p. 7 (Greek)

6.3 Strong, James. *Strong's Exhaustive Concordance of the Bible.* ©1890 James Strong, Madison, NJ p. 138

6.4 *King James Bible*, Revelation 9:1-2

6.5 Strong, James. *Strong's Exhaustive Concordance of the Bible.* ©1890 James Strong, Madison, NJ p. 76 (Greek)

6.6 *King James Bible*, Mark 5:10

6.7 Strong, James. *Strong's Exhaustive Concordance of the Bible.* ©1890 James Strong, Madison, NJ p. 78 (Greek)

6.8 Strong, James. *Strong's Exhaustive Concordance of the Bible.* ©1890 James Strong, Madison, NJ p. 77 (Greek)

6.9 *King James Bible*, Luke 8:28-33

6.10 *King James Bible*, Matthew 12:43-45

6.11 Strong, James. *Strong's Exhaustive Concordance of the Bible.* ©1890 James Strong, Madison, NJ p. 29 (Greek)

6.12 *King James Bible*, Matthew 8:28-32

6.13 Strong, James. *Strong's Exhaustive Concordance of the Bible.* ©1890 James Strong, Madison, NJ p. 14 (Greek)
6.14 *King James Bible*, Luke 10:17-20
6.15 *King James Bible*, Romans 10:13
6.16 *King James Bible*, Acts 2:21
6.17 *King James Bible*, John 3:16
6.18 *King James Bible*, Romans 10:9
6.19 Strong, James. *Strong's Exhaustive Concordance of the Bible.* (Comparative) ©1890 James Strong, Madison, NJ p. 60
6.20 Walker, J. Bartholomew. Wisdom Essentials ©2017 Quadrakoff Publications Group, LLC Wilmington DE pp. 198-204
6.21 *King James Bible*, Acts 19:13-16

7.1 Walker, J. Bartholomew. Wisdom Essentials ©2017 Quadrakoff Publications Group, LLC Wilmington DE pp. 58-61
7.2 Strong, James. *Strong's Exhaustive Concordance of the Bible.* ©1890 James Strong, Madison, NJ p. 118 (Hebrew)
7.3 Strong, James. *Strong's Exhaustive Concordance of the Bible.* ©1890 James Strong, Madison, NJ p. 71 (Greek)
7.4 *King James Bible*, Ephesians 2:8
7.5 Strong, James. *Strong's Exhaustive Concordance of the Bible.* ©1890 James Strong, Madison, NJ p. 77 (Greek)
7.6 Strong, James. *Strong's Exhaustive Concordance of the Bible.* ©1890 James Strong, Madison, NJ p. 77 (Greek)
7.7 Strong, James. *Strong's Exhaustive Concordance of the Bible.* ©1890 James Strong, Madison, NJ p. 77 (Greek)
7.8 Strong, James. *Strong's Exhaustive Concordance of the Bible.* ©1890 James Strong, Madison, NJ p. 77 (Greek)
7.9 Strong, James. *Strong's Exhaustive Concordance of the Bible.* ©1890 James Strong, Madison, NJ p. 24 (Greek)

7.10 Strong, James. *Strong's Exhaustive Concordance of the Bible.* ©1890 James Strong, Madison, NJ p. 385
7.11 Strong, James. *Strong's Exhaustive Concordance of the Bible.* ©1890 James Strong, Madison, NJ p. 24 (Greek)
7.12 *King James Bible*, John 14:12
7.13 Strong, James. *Strong's Exhaustive Concordance of the Bible.* ©1890 James Strong, Madison, NJ p. 32 (Greek)
7.14 Strong, James. *Strong's Exhaustive Concordance of the Bible.* ©1890 James Strong, Madison, NJ p. 47 (Greek)
7.15 https://www.merriam-webster.com/dictionary/erg (retrieved 8/10/20)
7.16 *Chambers Dictionary of Etymology*, Copyright ©1988 The H. W. Wilson Company, New York, NY p. 308
7.17 Strong, James. *Strong's Exhaustive Concordance of the Bible.* ©1890 James Strong, Madison, NJ p. 58 (Greek)
7.18 Strong, James. *Strong's Exhaustive Concordance of the Bible.* ©1890 James Strong, Madison, NJ p. 73 (Hebrew)
7.19 Strong, James. *Strong's Exhaustive Concordance of the Bible.* ©1890 James Strong, Madison, NJ p. 70 (Greek)
7.20 Strong, James. *Strong's Exhaustive Concordance of the Bible.* ©1890 James Strong, Madison, NJ p. 74 (Greek)
7.21 *King James Bible*, Romans 12:3
7.22 Walker/Quadrakoff. *Alleged Fantasy Volume I - Foundations.* ©2020 Quadrakoff Publications Group, LLC Wilmington DE pp. 382
7.23 Strong, James. *Strong's Exhaustive Concordance of the Bible.* ©1890 James Strong, Madison, NJ p. 330
7.24 *King James Bible*, Matthew 7:13-14

8.1 *King James Bible*, Luke 13:23-25
8.2 Walker/Quadrakoff. *Alleged Fantasy Volume I - Foundations.* ©2020 Quadrakoff Publications Group, LLC Wilmington DE pp. 87-88

8.3 *King James Bible*, Matthew 7:13-14
8.4 Walker/Quadrakoff. *Alleged Fantasy Volume I - Foundations.* ©2020 Quadrakoff Publications Group, LLC Wilmington DE pp. 90-92
8.5 Walker/Quadrakoff. *Alleged Fantasy Volume I - Foundations.* ©2020 Quadrakoff Publications Group, LLC Wilmington DE pp. 93-98

Embedded
Bibliography
(In Order of Occurrence)

OAI3 *King James Bible*, Revelation 12:7-9 (KJV)
OAI4 Strong, James. *Strong's Exhaustive Concordance of the Bible*. © 1890 James Strong, Madison, NJ p. 7 (Greek)
OAI5 Strong, James. *Strong's Exhaustive Concordance of the Bible*. © 1890 James Strong, Madison, NJ p. 38 (Greek)
OAI6 *King James Bible* Luke 20:36
OAI7 Strong, James. *Strong's Exhaustive Concordance of the Bible*. © 1890 James Strong, Madison, NJ p. 58 (Greek)
OAI8 *King James Bible* Revelation 12:4
OAI9 Strong, James. *Strong's Exhaustive Concordance of the Bible*. © 1890 James Strong, Madison, NJ p. 26 (Greek)
OAI10 https://www.merriam-webster.com/dictionary/nether ret. 11-18
OAI11 *Chambers Dictionary of Etymology*. Copyright © 1988 The H. W. Wilson Company, New York, NY p.597

OAI12 https://www.etymonline.com/word/hell ret, 11/18

OAI13 *Chambers Dictionary of Etymology*. Copyright © 1988 The H. W. Wilson Company, New York, NY p.525

WEIB17 *King James Bible*, Matthew 17:14-19

WEIB18 *King James Bible*, Matthew 17:20

WEIB19 *King James Bible*, Matthew 17:21

WEIB20 *King James Bible*, Matthew 17:22

WEIB21 *New American Standard Bible*: 1995 update. 1995 (Matthew 17:20) The Lockman Foundation: Lahabra, CA

WEIB22 *New American Standard Bible*: 1995 update. 1995 (2 Matthew 17:21) The Lockman Foundation: Lahabra, CA

WEIB23 *New American Standard Bible*: 1995 update. 1995 (Matthew 17:22) The Lockman Foundation: Lahabra, CA

WEIB24 *New American Standard Bible*: 1995 update. 1995 The Lockman Foundation: Lahabra, CA introductory pages, not numbered

WEIB 25 *The Holy Bible New International Version* © 1973, 1978, 1984 International Bible Society (Matthew 17: 20)

WEIB26 *The Holy Bible New International Version* © 1973, 1978, 1984 International Bible Society (Matthew 17: 21)

WEIB27 *The Holy Bible New International Version* © 1973, 1978, 1984 International Bible Society (Matthew 17: 22)

WENJAT24 *King James Bible*, Ephesians 6:17

WENJAT25 Strong, James. *Strong's Exhaustive Concordance of the Bible.* © 1890 James Strong, Madison, NJ p. 46 (Greek)

WENJAT26 Strong, James. *Strong's Exhaustive Concordance of the Bible.* © 1890 James Strong, Madison, NJ p. 58 (Greek)

WENJAT27 Strong, James. *Strong's Exhaustive Concordance of the Bible.* © 1890 James Strong, Madison, NJ p. 63 (Greek)

WENJAT28 *King James Bible,* Ephesians 6:17 John 1:1

WENJAT29 Strong, James. *Strong's Exhaustive Concordance of the Bible.* © 1890 James Strong, Madison, NJ p. 45 (Greek)

AF5.12 Strong, James. *Strong's Exhaustive Concordance of the Bible.* © 1890 James Strong, Madison, NJ p. 70 (Greek)

AF5.13 Strong, James. *Strong's Exhaustive Concordance of the Bible.* © 1890 James Strong, Madison, NJ p. 69 (Greek)

AF5.4 *King James Bible,* Matthew 7:13-14

AF5.17 Strong, James. *Strong's Exhaustive Concordance of the Bible.* © 1890 James Strong, Madison, NJ p. 979

AF5.18 Strong, James. *Strong's Exhaustive Concordance of the Bible.* © 1890 James Strong, Madison, NJ p. 63 (Greek)

AF5.19 Strong, James. *Strong's Exhaustive Concordance of the Bible.* © 1890 James Strong, Madison, NJ p. 58 (Greek)

AF5.20 Strong, James. *Strong's Exhaustive Concordance of the Bible.* © 1890 James Strong, Madison, NJ p. 34 (Greek)

AF5.21 Strong, James. *Strong's Exhaustive Concordance of the Bible.* © 1890 James Strong, Madison, NJ p. 979
AF5.22 Strong, James. *Strong's Exhaustive Concordance of the Bible.* © 1890 James Strong, Madison, NJ p. 36 (Greek)
AF5.23 Strong, James. *Strong's Exhaustive Concordance of the Bible.* © 1890 James Strong, Madison, NJ p. 72 (Greek)
AF5.24 Strong, James. *Strong's Exhaustive Concordance of the Bible.* © 1890 James Strong, Madison, NJ p. 15 (Greek)
AF5.25 Strong, James. *Strong's Exhaustive Concordance of the Bible.* © 1890 James Strong, Madison, NJ p. 14 (Greek)
AF5.26 Strong, James. *Strong's Exhaustive Concordance of the Bible.* © 1890 James Strong, Madison, NJ p. 259
AF5.27 *King James Bible,* Matthew 26:18
AF5.28 Strong, James. *Strong's Exhaustive Concordance of the Bible.* © 1890 James Strong, Madison, NJ p. 1107
AF5.29 *King James Bible,* Mark 14:4
AF5.30 Strong, James. *Strong's Exhaustive Concordance of the Bible.* © 1890 James Strong, Madison, NJ p. 35 (Greek)
AF5.31 Strong, James. *Strong's Exhaustive Concordance of the Bible.* © 1890 James Strong, Madison, NJ p. 34 (Greek)
AF5.32 Strong, James. *Strong's Exhaustive Concordance of the Bible.* © 1890 James Strong, Madison, NJ p. 79 (Greek)
AF5.33 Strong, James. *Strong's Exhaustive Concordance of the Bible.* © 1890 James Strong, Madison, NJ p. 58 (Greek)

Other Fine QPG Publications:

MEEKRAKER BEGINNINGS. . .

WISDOM ESSENTIALS—THE PENTALOGY

DONALD TRUMP CANDIDACY ACCORDING TO MATTHEW?

SHÂMAR TO SHARIA

IT'S NOT JUST A THEORY

CALVARY'S HIDDEN TRUTHS

INEVITABLE BALANCE

STATISTS SAVING ONE

OSTIUM AB INFERNO

REINCARNATION —A REASONABLE INQUIRY

QPG Publications are available wherever you buy fine books.

www.ingramcontent.com/pod-product-compliance
Lightning Source LLC
Chambersburg PA
CBHW031119020426
42333CB00012B/152

9781948219679